on the evolution of complex societies

*an anthropological series*
*edited by jacques maquet*

# other realities
volume six

*undena publications*
*malibu 1984*

on the evolution of complex societies
essays in honor
of
harry hoijer
1982

by

william sanders
henry wright
robert m<sup>c</sup>c adams

timothy earle, editor

*published for*
*the ucla department of anthropology*
*by*
*undena publications*
*malibu 1984*

Library of Congress Card Number: 83-51702
ISBN: 0-89003-139-8, paper; 0-89003-138-X, cloth

© 1984 The Regents University of California

Undena Publications, P. O. Box 97, Malibu, CA 90265

# CONTENTS

# INTRODUCTION

## Timothy Earle

This volume of essays *On the Evolution of Complex Societies* derives from the fourth series of the Harry Hoijer Lectures presented by the Department of Anthropology, UCLA, in the Spring of 1982. The subject for this series was settled on to illustrate the coming of age of archaeological analysis within Anthropology. In the past, many have viewed archaeology as a dependent subfield borrowing ideas from ethnology to make sense of the remnants of extinct cultures. No more. Technical and methodological innovations within archaeology make it now uniquely suited to study some of Anthropology's most fundamental questions. Archaeology's new role reflects its unusual long-term diachronic perspective and its ability to study societies unaltered by western impact. No where has archaeological research been so successful as in the study of the evolution of complex societies, one of Anthropology's central issues.

Archaeological studies on complex society derive in large measure from the seminal work of two scholars, Julian Steward (1949, 1955) and V. Gordon Childe (1936, 1943, 1951). Among North American anthropologists, Steward's ideas on cultural evolution molded an early consensus. Steward viewed cultural evolution as a process adapting a human population to its environment. To study the relationship between culture and environment, he concentrated on a group's settlement pattern—how a group distributes itself with respect to the landscape, changing patterns of aggregation and dispersion in response to resource availability.

For example in his famous Shoshonean example, he described how the yearly cycle of winter aggregation into camps and summer dispersed into isolated families was a response to changing patterns of food availability through the seasons.

Archaeologists picked up on the adaptationalist approach of Julian Steward, and much of the "New Archaeology" propounded since the 1950's has involved a working out of appropriate methods for investigating Steward's ideas with prehistoric data. Most important for studying cultural evolution archaeologically has been a reliance on the settlement patterns. In the 1940s, Steward helped design the Viru Valley project on Peru's north coast, in which Gordon Willey (1953) produced archaeology's first detailed settlement pattern study. Willey extended Steward's synchronic ethnographic description of settlement patterns to a long-term sequence of settlement pattern changes that records unambiguously the evolution of complex society in a single region.

A reliance on settlement patterns is a unifying theme of the work of Adams, Wright, and Sanders. Stimulated by Willey, Adams (1965, 1981) and his associates including Wright (1969) have produced a series of major settlement surveys which document the evolution of civilization in Mesopotamia. Also following up on Willey's work, Sanders (1965) conducted massive surveys in the Valley of Mexico and in other areas of Mesoamerica. In addition to refining methods of archaeological survey, his team has produced a remarkable record of long-term population growth as it relates to sociopolitical evolution (Sanders, Parsons and Santley 1979).

Similarities among the contributors are also strong in their methodological concerns. All three authors rely heavily on ethnographic and historical case examples to derive explicit models for archaeological evaluation. Sanders and Adams use modern and historic studies in demography to illustrate how demographic dynamics relate to culture change. Wright constructs his complex chiefdom model based on historic studies of Polynesian society and on recent archaeological data. Each author identifies key variables for investigation and then establishes how to study them with available data. Wright, for example, attempts to investigate variables related to symbolic control, tribute mobilization, and social stratification, indicating some of the recent development in archaeological research methods pioneered by Wright and his students.

Among the contributors to this volume, some divergence is, however, clear in their explanations of evolutionary process and these differences well illustrate the most important directions now being taken by anthropological archaeologists. Sanders with his explicit ecological orientation and focus on demographic factors is perhaps closest to Steward's adaptationalist orientation. Implicit in Steward's original notions is the progressive selection of improved cultural traits that gives a directionality to evolutionary change. This view of cultural evolution as progressive, however, is now largely discounted and is replaced by the more pessimistic view towards culture change, clearly articulated in Sanders's essay. For Sanders the evolutionary motor is population, the inherent growth of which drives up population density and gives a clear directionality and inevitability to cultural change. As population densities rise, the relationship between groups and their environment changes fundamentally with increasing resource scarcity, competition, and domination.

The paper by Adams sets forth a different, more eclectic approach to cultural evolution. Although population change is taken as an indisputable factor affecting economic and social variables, Adams considers the intricacy of the interaction among social, political, economic, and ecological variables. In his book, *The Evolution of Urban Society*, Adams (1966) explicitly rejects the central role of population and argues instead for the inclusion of the sociopolitical variables, especially social stratification and differential control of economic resources. Adams's work is part of a recent emphasis on sociopolitical variables which has been labeled "social archaeology." This new direction is often drawn in contradistinction to the adaptationalist work of Steward and of the "New Archaeology," and it looks in part to V. Gordon Childe for inspiration. Environmental variables are not dismissed but the complexity of causation in a cultural mileau is emphasized.

In the complex causal relationships considered by Adams, the importance of combining archaeological data sources and historical, documentary sources becomes evident. Adams argues persuasively for the integration of archaeological and historical research on cultural evolution in Mesopotamia. Where such documentary materials are available the insights of fine grained analysis are evident; where such data are unavailable, limitations are clear.

The paper by Wright falls generally into the school of "social archaeology" and bears similarities to the work by Adams. Working in Mesopotamia with an earlier time period and with a simpler society, Wright tries to recognize the importance of sociopolitical variables for understanding the operation and evolution of these prehistoric societies that precede the evolution of true states. Without the comparatively rich documentary materials available to Adams, Wright relies more heavily on cross-cultural comparisons. From this comparative data, he constructs a model of the functioning of a complex chiefdom which involves innovative ideas of ideological and economic control, and he tests this model archaeologically with his Mesopotamian data. Wright's work, as seen in his essay, is searching for means to study intricate evolutionary process with archaeological data. He suggests ways to use settlement pattern data and excavation data on architecture, ceramics, and the administrative clay seals to study social and ideological aspects of the evolutionary process.

In reading the essays by Sanders, Adams and Wright, I was struck by certain similarities. Although each emphasizes different variables, they agree that evolutionary process is causal, whereby changes in certain variables determine in a regular and predictable way changes in other variables. Evolution is something that can be described and explained, and the way to do this is to isolate the significant variables and to specify their interaction as systems (cf. Flannery 1972).

Differences are also clear. Sanders emphasizes environmental and biological variables as creating the main dynamic of change;

sociopolitical variables are more derivative with the infrastructure determining the structure. In contrast, Adams and Wright place more emphasis on the significance of the sociopolitical organizations determining dynamic interaction between groups in economic and other cultural ways. These two approaches—the adaptationalist approach of Steward and the more sociopolitical approach of Childe—may not be contradictory. Adams and Wright would not deny the important role of population and adaptational relationships; however, they would see them as only part of a more complex system of relationships. Sanders would certainly not deny the importance of the social structure but would question its independent role in shaping evolutionary change.

We appear to be dealing with a problem more of the level of analytical detail than of substantial differences in approach. The settlement pattern data utilized by Sanders is necessarily quite general, using relatively long time periods to recognize basic correlations among his variables. Adams and Wright, using more detailed data sources, urge a careful consideration of systematic interaction over the short run. As anthropological research on the evolution of complex society continues into the 1980s, I expect a new synthesis to develop which recognizes the long-term evolutionary patterns as explicated by Sanders but paying additional attention to the short-term mechanisms of change as explicated by Adams and Wright.

## References

Adams, Robert McC.
1965    *Land behind Baghdad.* Chicago: University of Chicago Press.
1966    *The evolution of urban society.* Chicago: Aldine.
1981    *Heartland of cities.* Chicago: University of Chicago Press.

Childe, V. Gordon
    1936    Man makes himself. London.
    1943    What happened in history, London.
    1951    Social evolution. London.

Flannery, Kent
    1972    The cultural evolution of civilizations. Annual Review
            of Ecology and Systematics 3:399-426.

Sanders, William T.
    1965    The cultural ecology of the Teotihuacan Valley. Uni-
            versity Park, Penn.: Dept. of Anthropology, Pennsyl-
            vania State University.

Sanders, W. T., J. Parsons, and R. Santley
    1979    The basin of Mexico: ecological processes in the evolu-
            tion of civilization. New York: Academic Press.

Steward, Julian
    1949    Cultural causality and law: a trial formulation of the
            development of early civilizations. American Anthro-
            pologist 51:1-27.
    1955    Theory of culture change. Urbana: University of
            Illinois Press.

Willey, Gordon
    1953    Prehistoric settlement patterns in the Viru Valley,
            Peru. Bureau of American Ethnology Bulletin 155.

Wright, Henry
    1969    The administration of rural production in an early
            Mesopotamian town. Museum of Anthropology, Uni-
            versity of Michigan Anthropological Paper 38.

# PRE-INDUSTRIAL DEMOGRAPHY AND SOCIAL EVOLUTION

William T. Sanders

A major question of social anthropology is the why and how of the evolution of social organization. The most important single question is the evolution of complex societies, societies that are large in size, internally heterogeneous, and politically centralized. The evidence from comparative ethnology, history, and archaeology is that this general type of social system has evolved from small, homogeneous, kin-based societies, what we anthropologists have traditionally called primitive societies, in a number of culture areas as parallel, historically separate developments.

While a number of theoretical paradigms may help resolve this evolutionary question, it is my contention that an ecological approach is likely to provide the most useful insights. The human ecosystem is composed of several subsystems, integrated in a complex web of relationships. Among them are the human behavioral (i.e., the cultural), the non-human biotic, the physical environmental, and the human biological subsystems. In this paper, I will focus on the demographic aspect of the human biological subsystem and its relationship to social evolution prior to the Industrial Revolution. The discussion falls into three main parts: the demography of pre-industrial populations, population behavior and social evolution, and population regulation.

*William T. Sanders*

## The Demography of Pre-Industrial Populations

In the energetic terms, all of the cultures that anthropologists have traditionally studied fall into a general type in which human muscular energy, fueled by food calories, was basic to the economy. It was on the basis of this energy resource that pre-industrial social evolution took place. The industrial revolution produced the first major change in the energetics of the human ecosystem and revolutionized human biology as well, particularly demographic behavior.

In order to understand the relationships between demographic and social behavior in pre-industrial times, therefore, we must first describe the characteristics of pre-industrial demographic behavior. From what data sources do we generate this description? Some years ago, Paul Baker and I dealt with this question in a seminar on human ecology. Our first step was to summarize and discuss the vast literature produced by sociology on the subject, with its greater depth and breadth in demography than our own discipline, in terms of techniques, data, and theory. An added advantage of using sociological data was that it was based on large samples, often national-level statistics.

On the basis of these studies, one can define three major demographic patterns simply in terms of crude fertility, crude mortality, and growth rates. One pattern, the western industrial pattern, is characterized by low fertility, 15 to 22 births per thousand per year, and low mortality, from 7 to 13 deaths per thousand. The model doubling rates of such populations range from 100 to 200 years. The low fertility is due to consciously applied techniques to prevent ovulation, fertilization, or fetal completion. The low mortality is a product of advanced medical techniques, resulting in epidemic controls and a reduction of infant mortality. At the other end of the spectrum are essentially agrarian nations, particularly in tropical Asia and Africa, where fertility is high (in the 40's or 50's per thousand per year), mortality modest (between 20 and 30), and where the population is doubling every 30 to 40 years. The high rate of fertility is the product of non-regulation, and the moderate mortality is due to the inefficient diffusion of modern medical techniques. Finally, a group of developing nations (Mexico is a primary example) share a fertility as high as the agrarian nations, a mortality comparable to western industrial nations, and a resulting doubling rate of 20 to 30 years. These are all nations undergoing rapid industrialization but where the peasant sector is still economically and numerically important. Implied in the classification, and verified by historical data, populations begin with an agrarian pattern, then shift ultimately to the industrial pattern. This process is referred to as the demographic transition. Implicit in this reconstruction is that fertility was high in pre-industrial agrarian societies, that the initial effect on population of the industrial revolution was to reduce mortality, and at a much later phase effective checks on fertility began to develop.

Of the three patterns, clearly the agrarian would be most appropriate for pre-industrial societies, but there is an obvious problem. On the basis of historical and archaeological data, which are discussed in more detail later, growth rates of pre-industrial populations were much slower than the 30-40 year doubling rate of twentieth century agrarian nations. Generally our estimates range from 200 to 300 years for relatively large areas (for example, areas over 200 or 300 square kilometers) for relatively long periods of time (for example, over 500-1000 years). We then turned to a series of anthropological studies of primitive populations, reasoning that these would more closely resemble pre-industrial societies. One immediate problem was the fact that sample sizes were small, a product of the fact that they were small "egalitarian homogeneous" societies. Nevertheless, the great number of such studies, consistency of the results, and the availability of techniques for statistically handling small populations revealed a clear pattern. All except nomadic hunters had fertility comparable to modern agrarian nations, but mortality was still too low, and so populations were doubling at roughly the rate of agrarian nations. One explanation is that, although they are isolated from modern medical resources, they are partly protected from epidemics by surrounding immunized peasant populations. Clearly then to get a more accurate picture of the demographic behavior of pre-industrial societies, we would have to obtain the data directly from them. This meant the use of archaeological data with their inherent problems and deficiencies.

Perhaps the easiest and most reliable statistic that can be obtained from archaeological data is the growth rate. This is because it can be generated from large-scale surface surveys, hence resolving the major archaeological problem of sampling. Complete surveys can be conducted over an area of hundreds, or even thousands, of square kilometers, sites can be dated from surface collections, and a history of human occupation can be obtained for hundreds, or even thousands, of years at a relatively low cost (Sanders, Parsons and Santley 1979). While absolute population figures are exceedingly difficult to generate from these data, relative population size by phase is fairly uncomplicated as a method. (I will not go into the methodological procedures and problems and refer the reader to various recent studies of this type.) Surveys have been completed for many areas and show quite similar patterning. Generally occupation begins with an initial colonization by a farming population, and is followed by a long period of sustained growth (Fig. 1). While the rates vary considerably, when calculated for short periods of time and for small areas, when large areas and considerable blocks of time are used, the variation is much less, with doubling rates varying from 200-300 years. This is an annual increase of only .2 to .3 percent, or an excess of only 2-3 births over deaths per thousand! In some profiles, this growth may be followed by a precipitous decline, by a period of stabilization involving minor fluctuation around a mean, close to the figure at the end of the period of growth, or slightly higher. In at least one case, the profile from the Basin of Mexico, this period of stability is followed by a second phase of rapid growth comparable to the early growth phase. Considering the fact that fertility is consistently high in all of the twentieth century populations, other than that of Western industrial nations, what the data suggest is that the much slower rate of growth is due to a much higher mortality than found in any twentieth century population.

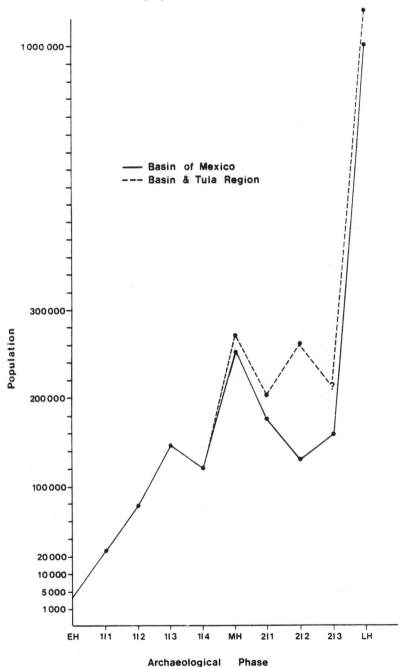

FIGURE 1

**Population History of the Basin of Mexico**
(From Sanders, Parsons and Santley 1979)

This conclusion is supported by evidence from paleo-demography, the analysis of skeletal remains from archaeological sites. While fertility rates clearly cannot be generated directly from such studies, a life table and survivorship curve can, and from this, a clear picture of mortality emerges. The major problem with the data is sample size; nevertheless, the pattern is remarkably consistent. Mortality was much higher than in contemporary populattions. The resulting model of normal pre-industrial population behavior seems clear. Fertility and mortality rates generally were both in the 40's and during periods of growth, rates of doubling were between 200 and 300 years. It is also clear from the data that even minor fluctuations in the relative ratio of the variables (births and deaths) can produce population decline, growth, or stabilization.

Before discussing the relationship between the demographic model and social evolution, I will digress to make some additional observations that refer to average nuclear family size. Considering the growth rates we have generated from settlement surveys and survivorship curves from osteological evidence (most particularly the very high infant mortality), it seems obvious that the average nuclear family size, particularly for the bottom of the social pyramid in stratified societies must have been low, considerably below average nuclear family size in twentieth century peasant populations. The completed fertility of the average woman would have been comparable, with the difference lying in the survivorship of children. A census of such populations taken in a given year would show an average nuclear family size of not much more than four people. One would also expect a direct correlation between social class and nuclear family size, the reverse to that which is found in industrial societies. In the latter case, the higher the family status, the lower the family size because the number of surviving offspring is the product of controlled fertility and is a conscious economic decision. In pre-industrial societies, the number of surviving children is based on differential mortality and nutrition, and health conditions would be more favorable to survival in the upper levels of the social system. The census of England from the first half of the eighteenth century, prior to the effects of the Industrial Revolution, dramatically illustrates this pattern (Table 1). One reason why I stress this point is that so many archaeologists utilize average family size from twentieth century peasants as a basis of calculating ancient populations.

I am referring here to the nuclear family, which tends to be the residential unit or household today. In many agrarian societies, however, several nuclear families often reside together in an extended family compound, physically expressed as a cluster of houses. The question then, in terms of estimating populations, is, how do the nuclear families that make up the extended family

### TABLE 1
### England in the Early 18th Century, Occupation and Family Size

| SOCIO-ECONOMIC CATEGORIES | FAMILIES | POPU-LATION | AVERAGE FAMILY SIZE |
|---|---|---|---|
| Aristocracy | 180 | 6,900 | 38.0 |
| Nobility | 16,400 | 146,600 | 8.9 |
| Officials and Functionaries | 10,000 | 70,000 | 7.0 |
| Businessmen and Shippers | 10,000 | 64,000 | 6.4 |
| Clerks and Professionals | 35,000 | 200,000 | 5.7 |
| Tradesmen | 30,000 | 125,000 | 4.2 |
| Artesans | 60,000 | 240,000 | 4.0 |
| Land Holders and Tenants | 310,000 | 1,690,000 | 5.5 |
| Laborers and Servants | 364,000 | 1,275,000 | 3.5 |
| Villagers With insufficient Land | 400,000 | 1,300,000 | 3.2 |
| | 1,235,580 | 5,100,000 | 4.1 |

Generalized Breakdown

| | | |
|---|---|---|
| Agricultural | 50% | (Some of urban laborers actually worked on farms) |
| Urban Workers | 37% | (Craftsmen only 5%) |
| Nobles, Officials | 4% | |

relate to the architectural complex? Clues to the utilization of structures by such families can be obtained by analogy with twentieth century populations where extended families still function, but one must always reduce the number of surviving children before adapting such figures for pre-industrial populations.

A common cultural characteristic of pre-industrial stratification is polygamy, with a close correlation between the status of a man and the number of his wives. An interesting question here is the possibility of consistent ratios of such households among societies of this type. A study of five West African complex societies (Hausa, Ibo, Yoruba, Ashanti, and Baganda) shows a patterning in which men with no wives or one wife make up 50-60% of the population, men with two wives 25-30%, three wives 6-12%, and over three 4-5%. The range is relatively narrow from group to group, suggesting an interplay of a few factors in such systems of social stratification (probably including the sex ratio, potential economic resources, pattern of political status, etc.).

Another important demographic feature of pre-industrial complex societies, even the more urban ones, is the dominance of the agrarian component numerically. This is clear whether one simply estimates the number of people by recognized occupational categories, or uses a more accurate means of calculating the amount of economic time spent at various tasks. (We have included here the case of the town of Huexotzingo in Central Mexico in the sixteenth century, and England in the eighteenth century as examples of simple censuses by occupational categories), (Table 1,2). Huexotzingo is representative of many pre-industrial complex societies in which virtually all work was accomplished with human energy; 18th Century England represents perhaps the technologically most complex society prior to the Industrial Revolution. The range of the percentage of the population classifiable as food producers is from 59-70%, a relatively narrow range considering the differences in technology. Of particular interest is the low percentage of the merchant—craftsmen elements—from 17-14%.

Pre-industrial societies were essentially agrarian societies and had essentially agrarian economies; therefore, differential land

## TABLE 2
### Social and Economic Status at
### Huejotzingo, Mexico, in 1560

| | HEADS OF HOUSEHOLDS | % |
|---|---|---|
| Nobles | 1101 | 12.0 (of total sample) |
| Commoners | 7985 | 88.0 (of total sample) |
| Clients of Nobles | 5510 | 69.0 (of commoners) |
| Farmers | 4375 | 79.4 (of clients) |
| Artesans | 1081 | 19.6 (of clients) |
| Merchants | 54 | 1.0 (of clients) |
| Free Commoners | 2475 | 31.0 (of commoners) |
| Farmers | 2013 | 81.4 (of free commoners) |
| Artesans | 137 | 5.5 (of free commoners) |
| Merchants | 325 | 13.1 (of free commoners) |

| Summary | | |
|---|---|---|
| Nobles | 1101 | 12.0 |
| Farmers | 6392 | 70.0 |
| Merchants | 379 | 4.0 |
| Artesans | 1218 | 13.0 |

control is likely to have been the most important economic factor in the evolution of social stratification and political centralization. The reason for the high ratio of food producers probably lies in a number of conditions: the basic technological needs of the population were small and required only a small class of specialist producers to satisfy them; agricultural energetics, especially with hand tools, were relatively inefficient; and transport technology was poorly elaborated. All of these factors made for a highly localized economy in which the bulk of the population were self-sufficient food-producers.

*William T. Sanders*

## Population and Social Evolution

The fundamental point of departure of the following discussion is that increasing complexity, social evolution, is essentially a detrimental one in terms of the standard of living and the personal independence of the large farming class at the base of the pyramid. This is the product of three factors. The first is the increasing cost of rent paid in the form of labor or goods as society becomes more stratified. There is also increased cost in what Wolf (1966) calls the "maintenance fund" as farmers' technological needs expand, a need demanded by increased intensification of land use. Finally, and perhaps the most important, the process of social evolution is directly and functionally related to population growth; and agricultural intensification, in most cases, costs more labor and results in a degradation of the resource base. The essential question then is, why do so many people accept from a few a social contract that is clearly disadvantageous? The only conceivable answer is that it is not a matter of choice, but the process that leads to stratification and the state is coercive, mechanistic, and highly predictive. A number of demographic factors and conditions operate to stimulate the civilizational process; population size, population density, and population growth.

First, it seems obvious, and I believe few anthropologists would question, that the size of a society is closely and functionally related to its organizational characteristics. Service's (1962) bands, tribes, chiefdoms, and states are closely correlated with modes and ranges of societal size: most bands have populations of a few score; tribes have modal populations in the hundreds, with confederations of tribes in some cases reaching into the thousands; stable chiefdoms have populations of a few thousand, but charismatic chiefs may temporarily create paramouncies which include ten thousand or more people. States, on the other hand, may include populations in the hundreds of thousands or even millions.

This shift in organizational characteristics and principles, as a society increases in size, is a mechanistic process related to the need to resolve intra-group conflicts, wage war, and organize economic relationships. In order for these functions to be carried out on an increasing scale, two organizational techniques become necessary: (1) a hierarchical mode of information transfer and decision making, and (2) a departmentalization of functions. While these relations, i.e., societal size and societal organization, should be well understood, only Carneiro (1967) and Naroll (1956) have actually tested the relationship. Unfortunately, both have limited their studies to single community societies. I say unfortunately because there is obviously a relationship between the size of the society and the proliferation and hierarchicalization of spatial communities.

Having accepted the functional relationship between societal size and organization, the next question is, why do larger societies form, given the excessive cost to most of the members? Clearly, population growth must occur for a society to increase in size but population growth equally could lead to dispersion and expansion of excess population over the landscape. The result would be to replicate small groups dispersed over a larger territory, and this is a well-known ecological process. Under such demographic conditions, considering the low effectivity and efficiency of early communication and transport technology, it would be difficult to integrate widely-spaced communities into a single social system and the result would be the persistence of small homogeneous social systems. In order for larger societies to form, the process of growth must lead to an increasing density. In fact, all ancient states have compact, closely-settled core areas. In some areas, this has even involved an effort by states to coerce subject peoples to resettle near the centers of administration (see Adams's discussion of walled cities in Mesopotamia).

Even accepting these strictures as to the relationships between population growth, circumscription, increased density, and increased efficiency of integration, it still leaves unanswered the question of why large social groups form, even with increasing density. Theoretically, population growth could still result in more small societies living in a decreasing amount of space occupied per society, rather than one of increased societal size. In other words, increasing density permits the formation of large societies, but it does not by itself explain it. Increased density must itself have an effect on social interaction and trigger mechanisms to change the structure of such relationships. To approach this question, I will first digress into a controversial issue in contemporary anthropology, that of the new theoretical paradigm of sociobiology, most particularly that aspect of it which deals with universal human characteristics and behavior, a subject generally tabu in anthropology since the discovery of cultural relativism.

A basic argument of sociobiology is that much of individual human behavior can be explained as a drive to maximize reproductive fitness. A derivative behavioral pattern is that of male power seeking, not only expressed in control over women, but, I would also add, over men as well. In more primitive societies, this competition is expressed directly and more physically. Men literally bully other men and accumulate women by force. In later stages of what is fundamentally the same behavior, economic institutions and mechanisms are developed to secure control over men, or rather their labor, and through them, over women. It is interesting that virtually all stratified societies either legally permit polygamy or socially accept it as a prerogative of rank. Accepting this point, then, there are *no egalitarian societies and evolution is simply an expansion of non-egalitarian behavior permitted by an increased opportunity.* To explain social evolution we must define the environmental factors and conditions that increase this opportunity. Since power seeking is a universal (I'm not sure that the maximization of reproductive fitness is entirely the story, but I have no real argument with biological reductionism in principle), one *does not need to explain non-egalitarian behavior, only the level of its success.*

The element in the environment that does change is the number of competing males per unit of space. The question then is, how does an increase in density cause a rise of opportunity, and what are the mechanisms by which humans use an increased density to augment their power? Social scientists have offered three convincing views—the conquest model, the conflict resolution model, and the agricultural intensification model. Carneiro (1970) has presented the most explicit statement of the conquest hypothesis, which may be summarized as follows:

1. Warfare is a natural condition of mankind, and, I would add, is an expression of the biological principles presented above.

2. Under conditions of low density, men organize themselves in small groups and fight against comparable groups to capture women, using primarily the raid and ambuscade. Such war parties normally involve only a few score and the results do not significantly alter the balance of power in the reign. Villages that do suffer heavily from such predation move and colonize new areas, a process typical of tribal societies. As we shall note later, there are also economic as well as purely political reasons for such moves.

3. As regions fill in with population through growth, distances between villages are reduced, and frontier areas are no longer available. Losers under these conditions cannot escape the penalty of defeat, and victors are able to exploit them economically.

4. Part of Carneiro's argument involves the notion of circumscription. He contrasts two types of environments, circumscribed and open, in which the potential for physical expansion is restricted in one case and unlimited in the other. In fact, what he refers to are simply differences in the size of the environment. In the long run, all environments are circumscribed and the process works anywhere with only the length of time varying. The concept, however, does explain precocity—why the coastal valleys of Peru, for example, achieved statehood by the time of the Spanish conquest, whereas in the Amazon Basin, the Indian societies at the time of European contact were primarily tribal in organization, or in their more complex manifestation, simple chiefdoms.

The conflict resolution theory, best presented by Robert Netting (1972), refers to a process of political centralization that
occurs internally within tribal populations in which armed hostil-
ity is absent or limited. His case examples are from Nigeria where a
federal government monopolizes the right to war and enforces this
right through a professional army and a police force. As population density rises, the problem of conflict of interest between individuals increases at an exponential rate even if we used a model in
which only possible paired conflicts (i.e., conflicts between two
individuals) were considered, and assumed that each pair would
only have one disagreement. The model does not begin, however,
to explore the potential of conflict since it does not include repeated conflicts between the same pair and various possible combinations of more than two individuals. Many of these conflicts
may be over trivial matters and not involve important goods like
women or land. Netting argues that there is a heavy energetic cost
to unresolved conflict and the conflicting parties in Africa today
often volunteer to surrender their autonomy to reach a solution,
even if it is unfavorable to one of the litigants. The individual
selected is, in his case studies, usually someone who already enjoys
certain prestige or influence; more specifically, he tends to be a
religious leader. Litigants pay him fees for his services, in some
areas cattle, and this economic gain is utilized by the priest to expand his economic power, and thus his political influence. In Flannery's (1972) terms, the position is promoted from one of relatively specialized and limited functions to a more general purpose
leadership. The economic wealth accumulated is also transferrable
to his descendants and the position (which often is hereditary any-
way) becomes fixed in a particular lineage or family. In essence,
out of this process, a chiefdom, in Service's terms, can evolve. The
surplus wealth enables the leader to give feats to attract political
male clients, to expand his household to include more women, and
hence, to increase the productivity of his own residential unit.

Boserup's (1965) position is closer to cultural materialism.
What she does is to show functional relationships between population growth, agricultural intensification, specification of land

tenure rights, economic specialization, and social stratification. Essentially, she argues that extensive agriculture is energetically (i.e., the ratio between work and crop yields) the most productive way of cropping under most environmental circumstances and the farmer makes a rational choice of how to use his land resources based on this ratio. As populations increase, farmers are faced with two options, migrating to frontier areas and maintaining an extensive system of agriculture, or intensifying production on lands already in use by reducing the fallow. Intensification leads to increased work per unit of yield, so that the energetic ratio becomes less favorable. She characterized the process in terms of stages — forest, bush, and grass fallowing, to ultimately permanent cropping, or even double cropping— although the process is, in reality, a continuous one.

As land becomes more intensively used, there is an accompanying process of increasing specificity of land rights, from communal holdings by entire villages to lineage rights within villages, and ultimately to private ownership of land. Along with this process comes increasing inequity in access to land as people perceive it as a potentially scarce resource and as investment increases in capital labor (physical improvements on the land, such as terraces, canals, etc.). The pressures created by these inequities lead to patron/client relationships, agricultural specialization, and non-agricultural specialization, all of which result in increased economic symbiosis or interdependence. The economic processes produce conditions in which politically and economically powerful families can increase their control and create political institutions to safeguard and protect their power.

There is no essential conflict between these three models of the effects of demographic characteristics on social structure and, in fact, they reinforce each other. I would add that economic variables tend to become increasingly important in the later evolutionary stages and that the more direct political factors appear throughout the process. The time required to achieve particular levels of social evolution should vary in terms of the size of the circumscribed space, as Carneiro argues, and with the rate of population growth.

In this brief paper I cannot go into detail on the evidential aspects of the population growth–social evolution theory, but will simply attempt to clarify some of the elements of apparent discrepancies on the empirical side.

First, there is a broad correlation between population variables and societal organization, whether we use a comparative ethnographic approach or a diachronic archaeological one. In the recent past—what Chapple and Coon (1948) refer to as the ethnographic present—there is an apparent correlation between population density and levels of social complexity. In sub-Saharan Africa, as an example, the densest populations and most complex societies are found in a broad belt extending from the Cameroons to the Atlantic coast, south of the Sahara, in the interlacustrine areas of East Africa, and on the Ethiopian highlands.

Archaeologically, where evolution from small egalitarian societies to large hierarchical ones has been documented, this is always accompanied by population growth. Although simple correlations do not of themselves demonstrate causal relationships the models of Carneiro, Netting, and Boserup provided the logical constructs as to how they interact.

It is primarily when one attempts to apply the approach to specific cases that difficulties and controversies arise. On the ethnographic side the problems may be summarized as follows:

1. There is no direct relationship between social complexity and *absolute population density figures*. In Nigeria, for example, the most complex social structure probably occurs in Hausa towns in northern Nigeria, while population densities are much higher among the institutionally less complex Ibo.

2. There are a number of cases where population densities are high but social evolution has not occurred beyond a relatively simply ranked society. Conversely, there are a number of cases of highly centralized political systems with only moderate levels of population density.

With respect to archaeological data, negative results seem to revolve around two points:

3. Periods of measurable changes, or rather high points in sociopolitical evolution, seem frequently not to correlate with periods of rapid growth, but rather with periods of stability in population.

4. Calculations of the carrying capacity of regions and measures of population sizes of prehistoric populations living in these regions usually show population levels well below carrying capacity; hence a population pressure model cannot explain social evolution.

In rebuttal, I would respond as follows. With respect to the first point, the theory predicts that people will alter their patterns of social interaction as their numbers increase. It is essentially *pressure on the resource base* that produces the changes. What this means is that each local situation is different in terms of what absolute numbers are necessary to produce a given level of pressure. In the case of Nigeria, for example, the Hausa are cereal cultivators in a high-risk, semi-arid environment and the Ibo are root crop cultivators in a low-risk, humid environment. The latter conditions allow for a larger, denser population in a region-wide sense. It should also be noted that, while regional densities are higher in Iboland than in northern Nigeria, the bulk of the Hausa population in fact is densely settled in a few favorable spots where irrigation resources are greater, and local densities are extremely high.

Point 2 is a more complex problem, but in part relates to my rejoinder to the first. Some economies, because they include sectors that require more space—for example, a pastoral sector—limit populations to moderate levels. On the other hand they may have efficient transportation technology—for example, animal transport—that makes communication more effective and hence permits wider spatial integration than with societies based on human transportation. In other cases the lack of correlation can be explained by an in-depth study of the history of the group, in other words, by a diachronic approach. Stevenson's (1968) rebuttal of Evans-Pritchard and Fortes' (1940) analysis of population density and degree of political centralization in Africa is a case in point. In the cases cited by Evans-Pritchard and Fortes, the analysis of the socio-political structure is the aboriginal one, but the data on population density and distribution is from the twentieth century. The history of several of the groups shows striking changes in population distribution from the past and furthermore the process is complicated by the imposition of a modern bureaucratic administration and by the adoption of new transport technology.

An apparent exception to the theory is highland New Guinea, where a native population, until recently little affected by western industrial economies, has experienced considerable growth (in some areas, populations densities are in the hundreds per square kilometer), but societies are still stateless.

In rebuttal, the comparative method and limited diachronic data available show *measurable* cultural evolution in highland New Guinea. Representing the beginning of the process are a number of pioneering groups characterized by low population density, who practiced long-fallow shifting cultivation. Distinctive of this exploitive system is a great variety of crops planted in a plot and a low, self-foraging domestic pig population. The human population resides in small dispersed villages, warfare is infrequent and the well known Big-Man, status-seeking social pattern is absent or weakly developed. With population growth, several things happen. Agriculture becomes more intensive with reduced fallowing periods; crop diversity is reduced; pigs are raised in increasing numbers and require increased agricultural production to feed them; warfare increases in frequency and scale; and political networks expand focused on the Big Man. At the end of the process are groups whose population density is in the hundreds per square kilometer, who crop the land annually, who grow virtually nothing but sweet potatoes of which over half is fed to maintain the pig herds, and whose Big Men control political coalitions involving several thousand people. While the social structure can hardly be described as egalitarian, nevertheless it is surprising that social structures of the chiefdom or state level have not evolved—in other words, there is an absence of macroevolution in the area.

The explanation lies, I believe, in two directions. First of all, it was not until the introduction of the sweet potato, a New World plant, certainly no earlier than the eighteenth century, that populations could expand generally over the highlands. We now have archaeological evidence of somewhat dense populations and intensive agriculture perhaps two thousand years ago; nevertheless, such areas must have been small, widely spaced, and limited to those valleys at lower elevations. The dense populations we see today probably were not achieved until this century, to judge from the fact that population is still expanding spatially into frontier areas. This means that the time factor is relevant; one hundred years or less is a very short time for macroevolution to take place.

I believe however that there is another reason—the energetic costs of the root crop-pig subsistence economy. Sweet potato cultivation in itself is time-consuming, particularly with stone tools, and to this cost must be added the production of food for pigs. While most New Guinea ethnographers have viewed pig production as a surplus activity, because of its association with Big Men and feasting, it is more reasonable to see it as a necessary element in a diet which is becoming increasingly based on sweet potato, a crop with virtually no protein content. If pig raising is seen as a necessary corollary of agricultural intensification and corrections in work costs are calculated in terms of neolithic technology, then the New Guinea subsistence strategy is a classic example of what Geertz has called agricultural involution, a process that leads to a steady decline in input-output ratios per capita. What the New Guinea case demonstrates is that other variables besides regional population pressure must be considered in specific cases. Interestingly, this other factor, per capita productivity, is an ecological variable.

With respect to the archaeological critiques (points 3 and 4) the problem is more complex and in part is methodological.

Archaeologists have the enormous advantage in testing anthropological theory in that they have control over time, but they suffer a serious disadvantage in that the processes we are describing must be inferred and not observed directly. The methodological problems of this inference are considerable. These include measurements of population size, estimates of carrying capacity, and the nature of the prehistoric political, social, and economic institutions. With respect to the supposed lack of correlation of the two processes of population growth and social evolution, in a number of cases the critics have not viewed it as process and have made carrying capacity estimates based on an intensive regime of cultivation, a condition which predictably, in terms of the theory, would occur only in the final phase of the process. More importantly, the characterization of some prehistoric populations as state organized is highly dubious; for example, the Formative societies of Mesoamerica, the late pre-ceramic societies of coastal Peru, or the fourth millennium B.C. societies of Mesopotamia.

Leaving aside the matter of accurate reconstruction, the question of synchronization of major events of the two processes is a more semantic matter. According to the theory, phases of growth in populations put stresses on the institutional structure of a population, stresses that in the initial phases are responded to by minor alterations in structure, but in the final phases can no longer be accommodated for except by major institutional breakthroughs. Is it therefore surprising the growth precedes major alterations in the organization?

Why populations should level off after the institutional breakthrough is not clear, but part of the problem may be the small size of the sample area. The achievement of new levels of sociopolitical organization is usually accompanied by spatial expansion of political organization is usually accompanied by spatial expansion of political orbits and is often accompanied by out-migrations from the core area. This may be a factor that resulted in a levelling off of population growth when Teotihuacan emerged in the Basin of Mexico (Fig. 1). It may also be that in some cases a carrying capacity is reached, at least in terms of available technology of food production and environmental conditions. The final spurt of growth, for example, between 1200 and 1519 A.D. in our Basin of Mexico profile, after a thousand years of stability, was permitted by the expansion of agriculture into the freshwater swamps of the Basin, and environmental conditions may not have permitted this in the earlier period.

## Population Regulation

Assuming that the previous theoretical argument is sound, i.e., that an increase in the density of human beings per unit of space changes the nature of their social interrelationships, and the exploitive strategies which they apply to their environment, and that these changes produce the structural and quantitative changes of social evolution, there still remains a critical question—that of the predictability or inevitability of the process. Do human populations necessarily increase in number and ultimately in density, or do regulatory mechanisms exist that keep human populations in some kind of balance with their resources? The final phrase, considering the dynamics of agricultural adaptation, is virtually meaningless. To clarify, the sentence should end with the phrase, in terms of an extensive approach to resource utilization. This is really what the population regulation position is all about.

Can and do human populations abort or retard the process described by Boserup of population growth, agricultural intensification, environmental degradation and changes in socio-political organization? If answered yes, then the variables that produce socio-political evolution must be sought elsewhere than the straightforward population growth—population pressure—social evolutionary model presented here. Some anthropologists, in fact, have taken this position (see Cowgill 1975) and I would say that cultural anthropologists particularly have tended to be much impressed with the stability of cultural systems and they have argued that stability is the norm. As they view it, population growth is the extraordinary phenomenon and needs to be explained. Some have even turned the argument around and see population growth as something engineered by leaders of certain kinds of political systems, most particularly state systems.

Perhaps the most convincing proponent of this position is Roy Rappaport (1973) in his paper, "Man, Nature and Culture," using a highland New Guinea group—the Tsembaga—as his model. His principal point is that ecological relationships are exceedingly complex, that humans are skilled observers who gradually accumulate ecological knowledge through experience, and that this experience is summarized in religious ideology. Much of what we describe as the ideology of a cultural system is therefore codified ecological knowledge. The belief system acts as a triggering mechanism to regulate environmental relationships through ritual. In the Tsembaga case, the two things that are regulated are the number of human beings and pigs per unit of space. Pigs must be sacrificed and consumed at regular intervals in the ritual cycle. The sacrifice is seen as a payment to the ancestral spirits of individuals whose death must be avenged by killing enemies, and as a reward to allies who make the victory possible. The effect of warfare is to reduce the resident population of both contending groups in the case of stalemates, and to displace groups in the case of victory. The periodic pig feasts accompanying phases of the warfare ritual cycle keep pig populations in check as well. Following Rappaport's argument, acquired ecological knowledge is encoded in ideology, and ritual acts as a thermostat to the human population and keeps it in equilibrium with its resources, in this case, with extensive shifting cultivation.

Aside from warfare, a number of mechanisms have been suggested by social scientists as population regulators, affecting either fertility or mortality or both; some are cultural practices, some are biological in nature.

With respect to fertility, these include either factors that reduce the risk of pregnancy or terminate pregnancies prematurely. Also included in the statistics of fertility, because of the secretiveness of the technique, would be infanticide. More properly, this is a mortality statistic. With respect to the risk of pregnancy, suggested

mechanisms are a conscious reduction of the frequency of inter-
course, periodic abstinence, retarded age of marriage combined
with strong sanctions against pre-marital sex, use of contracep-
tives, the practice of coitus interruptus, polygamy, and the requirement of celibacy for certain socio-economic groups within
the society. All of these fall under the category of cultural controls. Abortion would be a cultural practice prematurely termin-
ating pregnancy. Biological factors that affect conception or
successful pregnancy would generally relate to the physiological
status of the mother, primarily a synergistic relationship between
disease and nutrition, or the operation of one of these factors
alone. While not completely understood, there seems to be a relationship between fertility in women and the fat ratio of the
body. It has also been suggested that prolonged lactation retards
fertility, a factor which may be related to the fat ratio in that it
produces nutritional stress on the women. The combination of
diseases and malnutrition would also be a powerful factor in fetal
wastage.

With respect to mortality, disease and/or nutritional stress (in
its more extreme manifestation, starvation) are major factors
affecting the rate. Cultural practices such as warfare, child neglect,
human sacrifice, cultural responses to disease that may exacerbate
the condition (for example, reducing liquid intake of children
suffering diarrhea) have been suggested as population regulating
mechanisms.

My reaction to the notion of conscious planned population
regulation as a significant behavior in pre-industrial times is one
of extreme skepticism. First, it seems highly unlikely (and I will
develop this at greater length later) that people ever consciously
do anything to resolve potential long-term problems; generally,
human behavioral choices are responses to immediate problems
that involve immediate solutions. The notion that ecological
knowledge gets embodied in myth and ideology causing human
groups to respond in a subconscious way to environmental problems seems to be a mystical way of looking at man-environment
relationships, and, it is a proposition that is virtually impossible

to test. Furthermore, in order to validate such a hypothesis, one should be able to specify the mechanisms by which the encoding process occurs and no one has successfully done this.

Finally, there are vital reasons why humans should not control their numbers. On an individual level, farmers, particularly shifting cultivators—and this means most farmers over most of the history of agricultural man—need labor, and the only source of cheap labor for most farmers in pre-industrial agrarian economies is the reproductive capacity of the farming family itself. Considering the fact that agricultural intensification is the most common response to land pressure and the fact that intensification requires a high work input, high fertility is clearly advantageous to an agricultural household. The fact that the long-term effects of this process are disadvantageous is irrelevant; his preoccupation is with the immediate and short-term problems. On a group level, considering the fact that we have always lived in a competitive setting, reducing one's capacity to grow means reducing one's capacity to compete.

More importantly, there is no convincing evidence for significant population regulation. It is highly dubious that the cultural practices such as periodic abstinence, polygamy, class celibacy, coitus interruptus, or pre-industrial techniques of abortion or contraception have significant effects on fertility. With respect to mortality, I doubt that warfare, no matter how intense, has much impact on growth rates in primitive societies. Casualties tend to be primarily men rather than women and women in most cases are kept as captives. The Yanomamo, a primitive tribal group in Venezuela, are an obvious example of the non-effectiveness of this factor. The Yanomamo are described as intensely warlike and apparently 30% of the adult males die in warfare, yet their population is doubling every 50-100 years. Even the mass warfare of industrial nations has had a relatively minor impact on growth rates. All of the variables noted above probably have some influence on growth rates but in no sense can they be considered as effective population stabilizers.

In my opinion, the only cultural practices that may have

significant impact on fertility are retarded age at marriage and regularized infanticide. Added to these would be the combination of nutritional and/or disease stress on conception and successful pregnancy and the effects of disease and/or nutritional stress on mortality.

With respect to infanticide, this behavior has been reported for many human groups, characterized by a great range of socio-economic and cultural types, from hunters and gatherers to primitive cultivators to peasants. The major problem in analyzing the role of infanticide in population regulation is the lack of good quantitative data. Most groups are reluctant even to admit that they practice infanticide and in one primitive group, the Yanomamo, the function, at least consciously, is not population regulation. The fact that the Yanomamo population is increasing rapidly through time demonstrates that it has not had a long-term effect upon the growth rate even here. The Yanomamo, as several writers have pointed out, are an example of a cultural type, tropical tribal farmers, characterized by low population density, extensive resource exploitation systems, political fragmentation, and a lack of hierarchical organization. Warfare among such groups is endemic and the desire is to have male children to provide the manpower for the incessant fighting. Female children are frequently killed as a technique to raise the male proportion of the population. The practice probably does affect the sex ratio and growth rates somewhat, but certainly does not stabilize the population.

Infanticide, as practiced by hard-pressed peasant populations who see no additional labor gains to increased reproduction, but only increased costs, and some hunters and gatherers, particularly very nomadic ones, may be quantitatively significant either to retard population growth or to produce stability, but we have so little good data that it is difficult to assess the situation. Perhaps the most convincing data are from historical medieval England, where the practice of overlaying and the institution of the so-called orphanage (in reality institutions that functioned as slaughterhouses for unwanted children) may have had highly significant effects on growth rates.

Variation in age at marriage is almost certainly a cultural variable that has had a significant effect on fertility and growth rates [see Adams, p. 106] and the test case often cited is that of the history of the Irish population. Prior to the eighteenth century, the staple crop of Ireland was the European grain crop complex of rye, wheat, and barley. Crop yields in the humid, cool Irish climate, however, were low and viable farms had to be of substantial size. In the early eighteenth century, the Peruvian white potato was introduced. The crop yields are several times that of the European grains on the same soils, and hence a viable farm could be of considerably smaller size. During the next 100 years, the Irish population increased dramatically and average marital age dropped. Ultimately the population increase caught up to the productivity of the potato, age of marriage increased again, and populations began to level off in the nineteenth century. The implication of the above discussion seems clear. The only measures that function effectively to regulate population are *those that are themselves the product of economic or biological processes and severe pressures.* Thus, retardation of marriage and regularized infanticide seem to occur when severe resource shortages have already occurred and the process of intensification has reached something close to theoretical limits with a specific technology. Biological factors, such as increased disease and problems of nutrition, are also both factors that became significant when populations are pressing on their food supplies. What the operation of these factors means in terms of population regulation is that there is a finite limit to human population growth even with the extraordinary adaptive potential of culture.

At this point, I will return to Rappaport's case study of the Tsembaga, which seems to violate the conclusions reached above. In the first place, Rappaport never demonstrated that the ritual cycle of warfare and pig feasts regulated numbers of people or pigs. He offers no demographic history of either the pig or human population, and everything we know about the comparative ethnology of highland New Guinea makes this argument highly dubious. How does one explain the great variety of population density, agricultural practices, and level of intensification of land use in highland New Guinea groups, often within the same linguistic area, if mechanisms exist for maintaining populations at relatively modest levels? Are the Tsembaga unique? Most ethnologists (see, for example, Sorenson 1972) would see the comparative ethnology as representing stages of an evolutionary process in which the Tsembaga in 1962 are at the beginning of the process and the Chimbu, for example, are at the end.

In conclusion, while regulatory mechanisms obviously exist in human populations as in all animal populations, they seem to operate most strongly and most effectively when populations approach carrying capacity. A model used by biological ecologists (Fig. 2) suggests a process of gradually increasing environmental resistance as population density approaches carrying capacity. Human demographic behavior probably follows a similar pattern and hence, in principle, is similar to other animal species. This pattern is an expression of the Law of Biotic Potential and its adaptive value is clear; in an immediate sense it enables animal populations to colonize new areas rapidly and it expands the potential of a species for survival. What is unique with respect to humans is their capacity to modify their environment, which means that phases of growth become more prolonged and often seem the modal or normal pattern. The history of human colonization often occurs as a series of stages of growth and stability as new resource procurement technologies replace older ones. Arguing from this position, population growth is not extraordinary nor does it need to be explained—it is simply the operation of the Law of Biotic Potential. *What needs to be explained or defined are the factors and conditions that lead to stability.* In fact, this is the way ecologists have viewed the process all along.

*William T. Sanders*

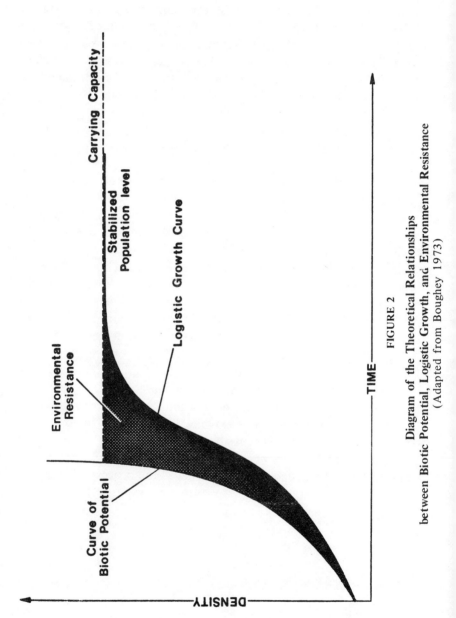

FIGURE 2

Diagram of the Theoretical Relationships
between Biotic Potential, Logistic Growth, and Environmental Resistance
(Adapted from Boughey 1973)

**Bibliography**[1]

Abernathy, Virginia
   1979   *Population Pressure and Cultural Adjustment.* New
          York: Human Science Press.

Allison, Anthony ed.
   1970   *Population Control.* Middlesex England: Penguin
          Books.

Arensberg, Conrad M., and Solon T. Kimball
   1940   *Family and Community in Ireland.* Peter Smith.
          Gloucester, Mass.

Blanton, Richard E.
   1975   The Cybernetic Analysis of Human Population
          Growth. In *Population Studies in Archaeology and
          Biological Anthropology*, edited by A. C. Swedland.
          *Memoir* 30. *American Antiquity* 40 (part 2):116-
          126.

Boserup, Esther
   1965   *The Conditions of Agricultural Growth.* Chicago:
          Aldine.

Boughey, Arthur S.
   1973   *Ecology of Populations.* New York: MacMillan.

Carneiro, Robert L.
   1967   On the Relationship Between Size of Population and
          Complexity of Social Organization. *Southwestern
          Journal of Anthropology* 23:234-243.
   1970   Theory of the Origins of the State. *Science* 169:
          733-738.

[1] The bibliography included here was used in writing this paper, but internal referencing was kept to a minimum because of the original oral presentation format for which the paper was prepared.

Chagnon, Napoleon
1968    *Yanomamo: The Fierce People.* New York: Holt, Rinehart and Winston.

Chagnon, Napoleon A., William Irons eds.
1979    *Evolutionary Biology and Human Social Behavior: An Anthropological Perspective.* North Scituate, Massachusetts: Duxbury Press.

Chapple, Elliot, and Carleton S. Coon
1948    *Principles of Anthropology.* New York: Henry Holt.

Cowgill, George L.
1975    Population Pressure as a Non-Explanation. In *Population studies in Archaeology and Biological Anthropology*, edited by A. C. Swedlund, *Memoir* 30. *American Antiquity* 40 (part 2): 127-131.

Dumond, D. E.
1965    Population Growth and Culture Change. *Southwestern Journal of Anthropology* 21:302-324.
1972    Demographic Aspects of the Classic Period in Puebla-Tlaxcala. *Southwestern Journal of Anthropology* 28:101-129.

Erlich, Paul R., and N. H. Ehrlich
1970    *Population Resources Environment: Issues in Human Ecology.* San Francisco: W. H. Freeman and Co.

Evans-Pritchard, C. C., and M. Fortes
1940    *African political systems.* London: Oxford University Press.

Fallers, L. A.
1956    *Bantu Bureaucracy.* Chicago: University of Chicago Press.

Flannery, Kent V.
1972    The Cultural Evolution of Civilizations. *Annual Review of Ecology and Systematics* 3:399-426.

Forseter, Robert, and Elborg Forseter eds.
 1969 *European Society in the Eighteenth Century.* New York: Harper and Row Publishers.

Galletti, Baldwin, and Dina Galletti
 1965 *Nigerian Cocoa Farmers.* London: Oxford University Press.

Howell, Nancy
 1976 Toward a Uniformitarian Theory of Human Paleodemography. In *The Demographic Evolution of Human Population*, edited by R. H. Ward and Kenneth Weiss. New York: Academic Press.

Lewis, T. M. N., and M. Kneberg
 1946 *Hiwassee Island.* Knoxville, Tenn.: University of Tennessee Press.

Lovejoy, C. O., R. S. Meindl, T. R. Pryzbeck, T. S. Barton, K. J. Heiple, and D. Knotting
 1977 Paleodemography of the Libben Site, Ottowa County Ohio. *Science* 198:291-293.

Mobley, C. M.
 1980 Demographic Structure of Pecos Indians. *American Anthropologist* 45:518-530.

Naroll, Raoul
 1956 Preliminary Index of Social Developments. *American Anthropologists* 58:687-715.

Netting, Robert M.
 1972 Sacred Power and Centralization: Aspects of Political Adaptation in Africa. In *Population Growth: Anthropological Implications*, edited by Brian Spooner, pp. 219-244. Cambridge, Mass.: M.I.T. Press.

Pirenne, Jacques
 1970 *Historia Universal.* Barcelona: Editorial Exito.

Pounds, N. J. G.
1975 *Economic History of Medieval Europe.* London: Longman Group Limited.

Rappaport, Roy A.
1973 Nature, Cultural, Ecological Anthropology. A *Warner Module Publication* reprint no. 799.

Sanders, William T.
1972 Population, Agricultural History and Societal Evolution in Mesoamerica. In *Population Growth: Anthropological Implication*, edited by Spooner, pp. 101-153. Kingbridge, Mass.: M.I.T. Press.

Sanders, William T., Jeffery R. Parsons, Robert S. Santley
1979 *The Basin of Mexico: Ecological Processes in the Evolution of a Civilization.* New York: Academic Press.

Schwerdtferger, F.
1975 Housing in Zaria. In *Shelter in Africa,* edited by P. Oliver. London: Barrie and Jenkins.

Service, Elman R.
1962 *Primitive Social Organization.* New York: Random House.

Smith, M. G.
1955 Economy of Hausa Communities in Zaria. *Colonial Research Studies* 26.

Sorenson, Richard E.
1972 Socio-Ecological Changes Among the Fore of New Guinea. *Current Anthropology* 13:349-372.

Stevenson, Robert F.
1963 *Population and Political Systems in Tropical Africa.* New York: Columbia University Press.

Ubelaker, D. H.
   1974   Reconstruction of Demographic Profile from Ossu-
          ary Skeletal Sample: A case study from the Tide-
          water Potomac. *Smithsonian Contribution to
          Anthropology* 18.

Weiss, Kenneth M.
   1973   Demographic Models for Anthropology. *Memoirs of
          the Society for American Archaeology* 27.

Wolf, Eric
   1966   *Peasants*. Englewood Cliffs, NJ: Prentice-Hall.

# PRESTATE POLITICAL FORMATIONS

## Henry T. Wright

It has long been evident that the first states—societies with specialized and hierarchically organized agencies of control—did not arise precipitously from a context of small independent egalitarian communities. Our nineteenth century precursors, relying largely on such sources as the Old Testament and classical myth or historiography, proposed that states developed from "primitive aristocracies," societies in a state of "higher barbarism" and the like. With the renewed spread of interest in evolutionary questions during the late 1950s, however, most scholars, relying on ethnographic accounts from Polynesia and Africa, conceptualized the antecedents of state organized societies as "chiefdoms." This social form was explicitly defined and discussed by Elman Service. For him, chiefdoms can be defined as "redistributional societies with a permanent central agency of coordination" (Service 1962: 144). His conception has served to focus much fruitful research; it has also been criticized for a number of reasons. Important for our understanding of state origins are the criticisms that (1) the taxon "chiefdom" includes societies of varying scale, among which only the more complex variants could become states, and (2) Service's emphasis on the definitional and explanatory importance of "redistribution" as a means of provisioning chiefly societies is not sustained by recent archaeological and ethnohistoric case studies. Timothy Earle has sought to resolve such problems by proposing a class of "complex chiefdoms" marked by "(1) discontinuity in rank between chiefs and commoners;

(2) specialization in leadership roles; and (3) increased centrality in the regional hierarchy" (Earle 1978:12). I have seconded this position, arguing that such a construct was a necessary element in a theory of primary state development (Wright 1977:381). In recent years there have also been many theoretically challenging case studies of particular complex chiefdoms, in both the New World (Peebles and Kus 1977; Helms 1979) and the Old (Renfrew 1973; Frankenstein and Rowlands 1978). It was thus surprising to read, in a recent review of the issue of chiefdoms by Robert Carniero, that "we still know very little about chiefdoms" (1981: 37). One could simply cite Carniero's own stimulating overview as refutation of his comment. Instead, however, I will emphasize a few recent insights which seem to me to point toward a unified construct explicating the variations in complex chiefdoms as pre-state political formations. (The word "formation" is used to emphasize that I am discussing systems of culturally constituted actions, rather than the actors' images of their "society.") Then I will evaluate this construct with evidence from Southwest Asia. First, however, some terms must be introduced.

For purposes of this discussion, a "chiefdom" can be recognized as a socio-political entity in which overall social control activities are vested in a subsystem which is externally specialized vis-a-vis other activities, but not internally specialized in terms of different aspects of the control process (e.g. observing, deciding, coercing); there is, in short, one generalized kind of political control. Within this set, however, there is a continuum of varying complexity. Simple chiefdoms are those in which such control is exercised by figures drawn from an ascribed local elite subgroup; these chiefdoms characteristically have only one level of control hierarchy above the level of the local community. The Trobrianders and the Tikopians are examples. In contrast, at the other end of the continuum, "complex chiefdoms" are those in which control is exercised by figures drawn from a class of people which cross-cuts many local subgroups, a "class" being defined as a ranked group whose members compete with each other for access to controlling positions and stand together in opposition to other people. Complex chiefdoms characteristically cycle between one and two levels of control hierarchy above the level of the local community (Wright 1977:381). The Hawaiians and the Natchez are oft-discussed ethnographic examples. These definitions differ from those previously offered, and some readers may object that a new definition demands a new term. The purpose of such terms, however, is to facilitate the selection of cases relevant to a particular theoretical problem. If a new definition results only from the clarification of an existing line of thought, as I believe this one does, then the further proliferation of terms seems unwarranted. The term "complex chiefdom" is not particularly poetic, but it has the advantage of being widely recognized.

The last of the world's complex chiefdoms were brought under state control early in this century, and the study of such developments is possible only with ethnohistorical and archaeological evidence. The recognition of archaeological examples of such socio-political entities relies upon the material consequences of the emergence of a chiefly class or nobility, members of which control generalized, polity-wide decision-making. We expect the following three features of spatial organization to be useful in identifying past complex chiefdoms.

1. Settlement hierarchy: the center of each polity in a network of interacting complex chiefdoms, usually the seat of the paramount, will become both larger than and architecturally differentiated from ordinary chiefly centers, both physically accommodating the paramount's following and providing a focus for major social rituals. There will thus be two levels of settlement hierarchy above the level of producer communities, though particular control activities may not have two levels of control hierarchy. When state organization with internally specialized control activities develop, they can be expected to take advantage of their capacity for greater hierarchy without fission, increasing span of control (cf. Johnson 1982:411-13 ) and generating more complex settlement hierarchies.

2. Residential segregation: While architecturally differentiated housing, albeit without vastly greater labor inputs, characterizes all societies with ascriptively higher-ranking domestic units, in complex chiefdoms with a discrete noble class there will be segregation by neighborhoods or in special communities of elite residences. We do not, however, expect palaces, built with mass labor inputs and providing spaces for specialized administrative activity.

3. Mortuary segregation: In addition to the more complex burial programs afforded ascriptively ranked individuals in simpler chiefdoms, we can expect that the noble dead will be isolated in death, as they were in life, close to areas of major ritual display. Unfortunately, in some societies, this may involve above ground maintenance of the corpse, such that it does not survive in the archaeological record, so mortuary evidence must be considered carefully.

In spite of practical problems with a single criterion, consideration of any possible case in terms of the three together should allow the recognition of a complex chiefdom as encapsulate in the construct discussed below. In the remainder of this paper I am going to attempt to synthesize three areas of recent research by anthropologists involving ideology, the control of production, and the control of the decision-making process itself. First, I will assess some recent research of these three aspects of chiefly societal operation. Then, these insights will be re-ordered and synthesized into a construct outlining the operation of complex chiefdoms. Finally, I will assess the evidence from the period immediately preceding state emergence in a portion of greater Mesopotamia to see how it corresponds to expectations derived from the integrated construct.

## Some Recent Research on Complex Chiefdoms

As mentioned above, the formulation of the concept of the "complex chiefdom" (Earle 1978) was in part motivated by re-evaluations of redistribution as a means of provisioning society as a whole. Such critiques contained various suggestions regarding the actual effects of chiefly redistribution, among the most intriguing of which were those noting that, while food and goods are extracted as tribute from producers, actual distribution is characteristically to lesser figures within the chiefly class, rather than to the whole populace, and that the redistributed items are often goods made by specialists, either part-time specialists locally supported by commoner production or full-time specialists supported by chiefs using some of the tribute extracted from producers (cf. Earle 1977; Peebles and Kus 1977:424-426). One can reason from this that if local production falters, then local subsistence producers would have to spend more time in more intensive food producing activities and less time on craft work. At first the movement of craft goods upward toward the paramount would decrease; if the crisis deepend, the flow of subsistence goods also would decrease. The first general material manifestation of a local problem would be a decrease in the exhibition of chiefly generosity to the lesser nobility and their followers (cf. Wright 1977:382). Similarly, decreases in the distribution of centrally produced goods would signal falloff in the paramount's income and therefore a deepening production or managerial crisis, and decreases in goods imported from other polities would signal falloff in inter-chiefdom exchange and thus diplomatic failures. Such deficits could be expected to motivate either chiefly reforms, internal rebellions, diversionary declarations of war on neighbors, or various other responses, depending on the particular local situation. Any of these actions would lead to a new adjustment between production and tribute demands. Thus, chiefly distribution of craft items and materials, at least among the complex chiefdoms, can be conceptualized as a mechanism regulating the tributary economy.

Is there archaeological evidence that such distributional regulation actually characterizes pre-state polities? In Mesoamerica,
there is evidence of redistribution in both the Early and Middle
Formative phases in the Valley of Oaxaca (Winter and Pires-
Ferreira 1976). There is also evidence of craft specialization, both
central and local (Flannery and Winter 1976). Is there evidence,
however, that the distribution of goods, among its other results,
also informed ancient Oaxacans about the state of their political
economy and, from their perspective, the competence of their
chiefs? There is some evidence that conforms with this proposition. For example, in a sequence of house construction and destruction incidents at the subsidiary village of Fábrica San José,
a drop in the quantities of imported obsidian relative to local
cherts is accompanied by burning of the house, suggesting that
redistributional failure is indeed associated with violence (Drennan
1976b:89, 206; Wright 1977:391). However, there are alternative
ways of interpreting these data, and broader studies explicitly
designed to evaluate the regulatory role of redistribution in chiefly
Oaxaca are still in the future.

If redistributional failure can serve to motivate war and rebellion and to adjust the relation between population, production,
and extraction, how does production and extraction ordinarily
proceed? In short, what is it that was being "regulated?" Working
with ethnohistorical and archaeological data from southeastern
North America, Vincas Steponaitis (1978, 1981) has recently
investigated this question. He was intrigued by a paper by Elizabeth Brumfiel (1976) which examined settlement sizes and the
productivity of settlement environs during Middle and Late Formative phases in the Basin of Mexico, in order to see whether the
correlation between population (as indicated by settlement size)
and productive potential of the environs increased with increasing
regional population density. In fact, she found a complex relation
in which larger centers seemed to have a far higher ratio of people
per unit of productivity than smaller centers (Bramfiel 1976:
Fig. 8-13). Brumfiel suggested that this was evidence that larger
centers were extracting or mobilizing subsistence products from

smaller centers. Steponaitis reasoned that such a tributary economy would give rise to settlement patterns different from the "central-place" patterns created in market economies. In tributary economies, in which bulky foodstuffs were extracted, the least costly location for an intermediate tribute gathering center would be somewhere between the local producer communities and the major seat of the paramounts. Local chiefs would here aggregate goods, take their share, and pass the rest to the paramount. Steponaitis predicted precise optimal locations for such intermediate centers based upon the tribute rates and other variables, and argued this to be the case in an archaeological example (Steponaitis 1978). Having elucidated the locations of centers in terms of the economics of tribute mobilization, Steponaitis (1981) turned to the specification of settlement sizes relative to local productivity as depicted by Brumfiel, constructing an elegant algebraic model in which the disparities between the productivity-to-population ratios of large centers versus small centers versus villages were functions of tribute extraction rates. To the extent that a center took a portion of each subsidiary center's production, it could have more people than its local environs could sustain, while to the same extent, subsidiary settlements must be smaller. Assuming locally grown maize to be the primary form of tribute, Steponaitis re-analyzed the Formative settlement data from the Basin of Mexico showing that the settlement sizes observed could be explained in terms of tribute rates of 15% to 22% (1981:343, 355).

With this construct for the operation of tributary economies, we still lack an understanding of the circumstances in which producers would willingly give up much of what they produce in the absence of the reciprocity inherent in a redistributional economy as conceptualized by many anthropologists, or of the coercion that is thought to characterize states. Such issues have been the special concern of ethnologists studying the ideologies of those few chiefly societies which survived into the 20th century, and of ethnohistorians working with 19th century documentary accounts. There have been many contributions to this area of thought; much of the discussion of "sacred kingship" in Africa is relevant to chiefly ideology. However I, like many North American archaeologists, owe much of my understanding of chiefly ideology, that is, the system of beliefs which motivates both nobles and commoners, to the writings of Marshall Sahlins. Sahlins (1963) long ago suggested that the social class divisions seen in chiefdoms such as those of the Hawaiian archipelago—cases with a highly ranked noble or chiefly class and a commoner class whose rank is minimal—must have developed from simpler patterns of ascribed rank such as those described for smaller Pacific island societies. He suggested that one way in which a noble class could have emerged was from the repeated re-definition of rank distinctions as communities fissioned and moved above (Sahlins 1977: 23). The increasingly far-flung relations among the ranking families, compounded as some individuals are exiled from their homes and others marry distant prestigious kin, must be documented with lengthier genealogical histories, in which exotic and even origins come to be emphasized. The ritual actions of the higher ranking chiefs, even their very existence, is thought to sustain the universe and nothing commoners could do can reciprocate adequately for the chiefly contributions (Sahlins 1981). No material recompense should be needed for offerings to chiefs in their ritual capacities. Food, the labor to build chiefly houses and shrines, and the sumptuary goods which mark them off from ordinary people all flow to the paramounts.

But how are such ideologies to be archaeologically documented? In the Americas, the development of the symbols of rank and their implications for chiefly ideology are widely discussed. In earlier Formative Mesoamerica, the wide distribution of objects fashioned with "Olmec" motifs (Benson 1968) represents such a development. Associated objects of magnetite, jade and other materials were fashioned in ways calculated to dazzle and mystify (Drennan 1976a:357-359). Individual objects, of course, have little significance; it is the occurrence of a complex of motifs and materials in a context of ritual use which can be used to test propositions about ideology. A more precise indication that a system of beliefs about cosmic power was operating is the existence of symbolizations specifying nobles and the major events important in their lives in terms of cosmic forces. In Oaxaca, representations of cosmic and natural elements develop in the Early Formative (Pyne 1976) and the naming of nobles with calendrical signs is firmly attested during the Formative (Marcus 1976:43-45; Flannery, Marcus and Kowaleski 1981). Such naming is the kind of cosmic association which can motivate participation in the tributary economies previously discussed.

These three elements can now be taken, not—as above—in the order in which they became important to my thinking, but in the dynamic order in which they come into operation, as chiefs expanded their ritual and political control of production, warfare, and other aspects of societal life.

## An Integrated Construct for Complex Chiefdoms

Neither the difficult question of why some societies ascribe the right to make community-wide decisions to office-holders drawn from a limited social sub-group, nor the question of why some networks of simple ascriptively ranked societies develop social classes are crucial to this essay. Regarding the latter question, it suffices to suggest that—if productive systems can sustain a continuity of the social network in time (and many cannot, cf. Leach 1954; Friedman 1975)—with time, intermarriages and disputes among the ranking families will disperse claimants to office. Many individuals may compete for offices with which few will have any local connection. Indeed, the ranking or noble class as a whole can be expected to oppose any local interests (cf. Bloch 1977). Thus, the development within a network of chiefly polities of a class competing for positions, but opposing others outside the class, may be simply explained.

Whatever the explanation of the development of a chiefly class, each family within it will have far-flung marriage alliances, very different from the local networks of commoners. Claims of geographically distant prestigious links or temporally distant divine links will be emphasized in the competition for offices. Once office is achieved, one's ritual prerogatives will be bolstered with claims to cosmic powers resulting from these links. As such claims to power become grander, the need to materially reciprocate commoners for their gifts become less, and "reciprocity" or "redistribution" can be transformed into tribute mobilization.

The centripetal flow of tribute must aggrandize the center, simultaneously giving the paramount the possibility of becoming more than a first among equals and making the other office holders permanent political and ritual subsidiaries. Two levels of control hierarchy are evident on each occasion that goods or people are marshalled for the paramount and his followers. The subsidiary chiefs' centers will be located to facilitate control with a minimum expenditure, main centers will grow in proportion to what paramounts receive and smaller centers grow no farther than the limits imposed by tribute demands.

A paramount's best strategy will be to keep administration as simple as possible. The fewer levels of hierarchy below him, the more difficult it will be for subsidiaries to rebel or make separate claims at his death. Ritual, extractive, and political activities are redundantly linked so that to undertake one is to do the others, minimizing need for administrative complexity. Productive activities are left as much as possible to individual producers and economic self-sufficiency is encouraged making exchange less frequent thus further reducing demand on the administrative capacities of the chiefs (Earle 1978:158-162). The success of the paramount in times of bountiful natural productivity and successful rule would be marked by an upward flow of consumables and status-related craft goods. Any diminution in the redistributing of such items will lead to claims of chiefly incompetence among sub-chiefs and chiefly followers. The wise paramount will attempt to reorganize production or to increase his income by seizing productive capacity from his neighbors; the unwise paramount, especially one who has been so foolish as to create more than two levels of hierarchy, will face assassination, fission, or rebellion led by other nobles who believe themselves to have better claim to the office of paramount. Whatever the outcome, nobility and commoners will be killed, political relations will break down, and the building process will start again.

This kind of system will have a characteristic pattern of centralization and decentralization through time. Brief periods of breakdown, occurring every decade or so—succession disputes, minor rebellions and small wars—are frequently observed ethnographically but will be documented only rarely with presently-used archaeological technique. Region-wide rebellions, civil war, and perhaps the replacement of one chiefly line by another will be expected after long and successful paramouncies during which chiefly families have multiplied and segmented, perhaps every century or so. The destruction and perhaps even the abandonment of great centers and changes in traditional chiefly symbolism should be evident to the archaeologists.

At this point, it would be instructive to evaluate this preliminary construct with evidence from a network of developing complex chiefdoms in the Old World very different from New World and Polynesian examples, the study of which has generated many of the propositions discussed above. Do we find evidence of chiefly claims to cosmic powers, tribute extraction justified by such claims, and regulation of such extraction by the variations in goods redistribution? The reader will see that such an evaluation will reveal both strengths and weaknesses in this preliminary integrated construct.

## An Illustrative Example: Southwestern Iran During the Late Fifth Millennium B.C.

By 4500 B.C., the productive patterns that still sustain many communities in the Near East were well established in southwestern Iran (Fig. 1). Specialized varieties of wheat and barley, irrigated in many lowland areas, were widespread. Lentils and other protein-rich foods were also grown (Helbaek 1969:405-412;

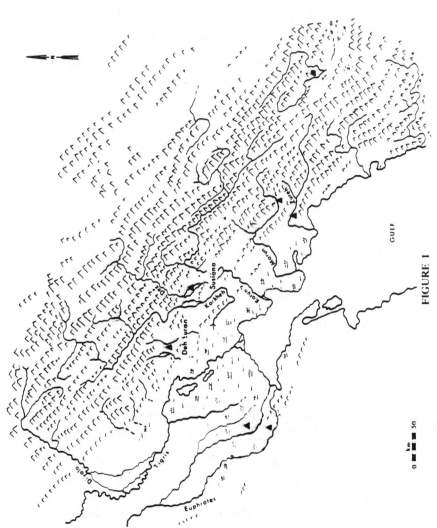

**FIGURE 1**

**A Map of the Southeastern Portion of Greater Mesopotamia
during the Middle of the Fourth Millennium B.C.**

Shaded areas mark some of the major settled areas; triangles indicate major centers.

Miller 1978, 1981). Sheep, goats, and cows were kept everywhere in varying proportions, probably in order to exploit them for their secondary milk and fiber products as much as for their meat (Hole, Flannery and Neely 1969:361-366; Redding 1981:239-259). Every valley with a few square kilometers of irrigatable soil had a small center and a few subsidiary villages or hamlets; larger valleys and plains had more complex patterns with centers covering up to 15 hectares, subsidiary centers of 3-5 hectares, and villages and hamlets of smaller sizes. Some plains may have had populations approaching 20,000 people (Wright and Johnson 1975:274-276). (Recently proposed criteria for population estimation [Kramer 1980:322-327], however, would lead to smaller estimates.) Many of the settlements—villages as well as centers—have evidence of craft production such as potting, chert knapping, spinning and weaving, or grindstone manufacture.

What kind of socio-political organization did Late fifth millennium societies have? I consider here the Farukh Phase of the Deh Luran Plain and contemporary phases (ca. 4600-4300 B.C.) and the Suse Phase of the Susiana Plain and the contemporary phases (ca. 4300-4000 B.C.). First, as noted above, there were central settlements often larger than all neighboring settlements combined. Also, as discussed later, Suse Phase Susa, the one major center extensively excavated, has evidence of a large central platform with distinctive decoration and a ritual building on its summit. Thus, major centers appear to be demarcated from minor centers in terms of size and symbolic features.

Second, there is some evidence that socially segregated housing was present. For example, at Tepe Farukhabad on the Deh Luran plain, two separate sequences of Farukh Phase housing were partially exposed (Wright 1981:12-22, 65-66). Both were sequences of buildings with outer compound walls and inner room blocks. Both had similar associated domestic refuse—ceramic vessel fragments, stone tools, and food remains. There were, however, differences between the two sequences. In one, houses were built of carefully laid mud-brick walls founded on mud brick platforms; these were carefully repaired and cleaned throughout their lifetimes. In the other sequence, buildings had casually laid walls founded on the leveled ground surface; these had little maintenance and were littered with debris. Furthermore a larger storage structure associated with the more elaborate buildings suggests greater control over the grain supply. Although the debris around the buildings in the two different sequences did not indicate significantly different bone discard, qualitative differences existed in the wild animals butchered, suggesting sumptuary rules defining access to animal foods (Redding 1981:253-254). Residential architectural differences exist also in separate quarters at other sites, some of which will be discussed subsequently. It is unfortunate, however, that no extensive clearance of larger portions of sites has been done to demonstrate that the contrasts noted occur in contemporary segregated quarters of the same community.

Third, mortuary ritual from cemeteries should be useful in assessing late fifth millennium socio-political organization. Unfortunately, only one cemetery of the Suse Phase Necropole of Susa (Morgan 1912) has been extensively excavated on the plains of southwestern Iran. Records of individual grave lots are not available for this early excavation, and Hole (1982) has recently shown that the evidence admits of several different interpretations.

Accepting the existing evidence of settlement hierarchy and residential segregation by rank, incomplete as it may be, as conforming to the existence of late fifth millennium complex chiefdoms, one may consider whether there is evidence of the kind of symbolic order, tribute extraction, and political-economic regulation proposed as part of the integrated construct.

While archaeologists cannot directly monitor a past class ideology—a system of beliefs about the relations between classes—we can certainly seek the material symbolic correlates of such an ideology. We would expect the members of the noble stratum to use specific symbols—in ritual performance, political action, and social display—which contrasts with those used by ordinary people in terms of the breadth of their reference and their evocation of control over natural forces.

For the earlier part of the period under consideration, the Farukh Phase of the Deh Luran Plain and the contemporary phase on the Susiana Plain, the sole extensive corpus of symbolic display is that of painted ceramic vessels. These appear to be of uniform stylistic complexity, without any subset of ceramics showing a more complex design grammar or distinctive use of symbolic elements (Pollock 1983). It is important to note, however, that no major center of these phases has been excavated. In the available small corpora of vessels from relatively small centers and villages, such special symbolism might be represented only by single vessels. Only with evidence from the major centers, both of ceramics and of other style-rich materials such as seals, could one fairly evaluate the quality of chiefly symbolism.

The evidence for the later Suse Phase—the Susa I or Susa A Phase of the older literature (Le Breton 1957:89-94)—is more diverse. Extensive excavation evidence is available from two sites, the small hamlet of Djaffarabad 1-3a (Dollfus 1971, 1978) and the major center of Susa itself (Morgan 1912; Dyson 1966; Stéve and Gasche 1973; Le Brun 1971; Perrot 1972; Canal 1978). Djaffarabad apparently had a series of small rooms around an open space (Fig. 2a). Susa, in contrast, had a large central two-stage platform of mud bricks, comprising about 570,000 cubic meters, surrounded by buildings of various sizes, open spaces, and cemetery areas (Fig. 2b). Both stages of the platform's south face had recessed corners; if such recesses were repeated on all four sides, the platform would have formed a complex cruciform. On the summit of the platform, eight meters above the surrounding settlement, was a possibly residential building with massive walls, rows of chambers of a type later used for grain storage, and a smaller platform with recessed corners decorated with representations of caprid horns, a later indication of a shrine (Stéve and Gasche 1973). The central architectural complex of the major regional center was apparently planned as a series of nested cruciform constructions.

A large series of stamp seals and sealings available from Susa can be attributed to this period (Amiet 1972:I/5-34, II/Plates 38-58).

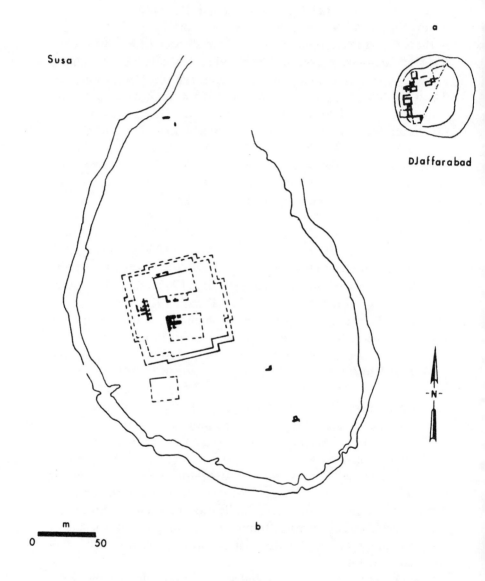

FIGURE 2

**Known Features of Suse Phase Djaffarabad and Susa Represented at the Same Scale**
(Sources: a. Dollfus 1978:Fig. 7; b. Canal 1978:Figs. 1,9; Stéve and
Gasche 1973:foldout; Dyson 1966:Plates LVII-LIX; Le Brun 1971,Fig. 31)

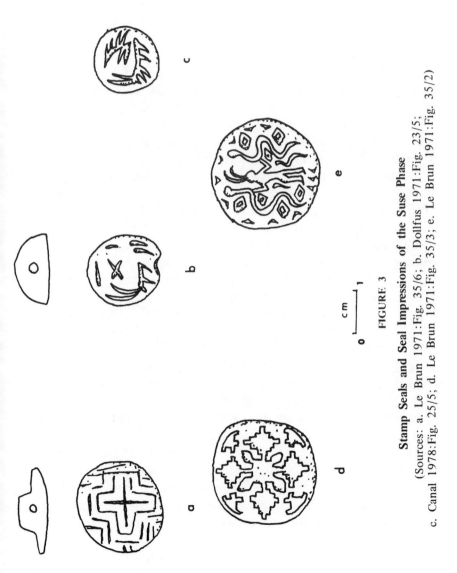

**FIGURE 3**

**Stamp Seals and Seal Impressions of the Suse Phase**

(Sources: a. Le Brun 1971:Fig. 35/6; b. Dollfus 1971:Fig. 23/5;
c. Canal 1978:Fig. 25/5; d. Le Brun 1971:Fig. 35/3; e. Le Brun 1971:Fig. 35/2)

The more common are the simple seals with crossed grooves and simple animals, typically caprids (Fig. 3b, 3). Less common, comprising only 9% of the seals, are seals with more complex representations. One common complex seal form is the "master of animals" (Fig. 3e, Amiet 1972:I/28; cf. Miroschedji 1981), a figure holding animals such as snakes or fishes in outstretched arms. Another complex representation is a nested cruciform, sometimes within a circle, usually with four similar geometrical arrangements at the four extremities (Fig. 3d). The nested cruciforms suggest the plan for the central platform of Susa.

The most diverse source of symbolic representations are the painted ceramic bowls and jars (Fig. 4). Many of the motifs continue from the earlier phases, but some vessels, particularly the large conical goblets, and small bowls and jars found in mortuary contexts at Susa and in domestic contexts at Susa and smaller sites, have more complex rules of design formation and often are more careful design drafting (Pollock 1983). One can argue that such design complexity is related to numbers and kinds of sociopolitical distinctions. Of particular importance discussion are certain motifs in circles (Fig. 4g, h) subsidiary to the main motif, often an ancient and widely-used motif such as the caprid. A common variant among these added circles is a cruciform motif, similar to the motifs on some complex seals and to the plan of Susa's central building (Fig. 4h). While this symbolic usage requires verification in the context of a comprehensive study of Suse Phase iconography, such as that now being undertaken by Frank Hole (1982), it is certainly suggestive of the widespread use of a hithertofore rare symbolism in ritual performances at the center of Susa, in political action in the control of goods storage and movement, and in social display on special craft goods. This is conformable with the proposition that there would be a distinctive material marking of the noble class. Evaluation of the cosmic referents of the elite iconography, however, awaits study of the developing system of style elements throughout the Susiana ceramic tradition, such as that now being completed by Genevieve Dollfus.

Tribute extraction in the New World, as mentioned above, has

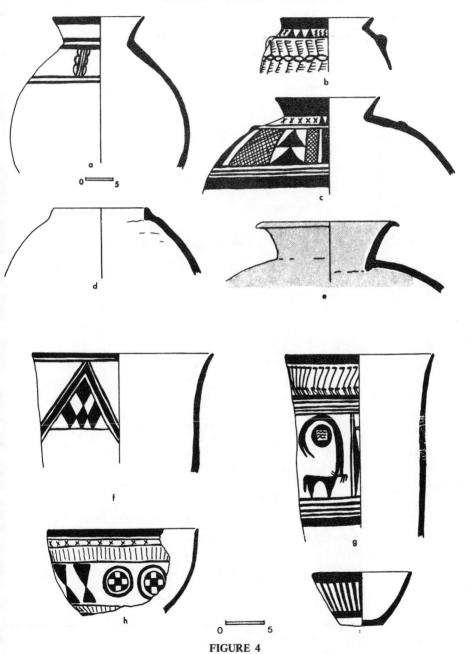

**FIGURE 4**
Ceramics of the Suse Phase from Djaffarabad
(Sources: a. Dollfus 1971:Fig. 18/4; b. Dollfus 1971:Fig. 16/9; c. Dollfus 1971:Fig. 17/6;
d. Dollfus 1971:Fig. 15/5; e. Dollfus 1971:Fig. 19/2; f. Dollfus 1971:Fig. 14/6;
g. Dollfus 1971:Fig. 14/2+9; h. Dollfus 1971:Fig. 11/6; i. Dollfus 1971:Fig. 12/5)

been studied indirectly through its effects on settlement patterns, particularly the location and size of the subsidiary centers. In southwestern Iran, we find that subsidiary centers—sites such as Farukhabad that differ from hamlets and villages *both* in being relatively larger and in having remnants suggestive of massive and specialized architecture—are in the locations indicated by the Steponaitis tributary model. On the Deh Luran Plain, for example (Fig. 5), Farukh Phase Farukhabad is not located in the midst of the village cluster westward from the major center of Musiyan. Rather it is between this cluster and Musiyan. The Suse Phase centers on the Susiana Plain have a similar, albeit more complicated, distribution (Fig. 6). Each cluster of small settlements has a subsidiary center on its edge closest to Susa. There are, however, other subsidiary centers not clearly associated with smaller settlements, such as the three newly founded centers on the west and south edges of the plain. These seem most likely to have been border centers, located for reasons of defense or exchange with nomads. On the other hand, we do not find that the relation between settlement size and the productivity of its environs conforms to that predicted by Steponaitis's formulation. As one can see on Figure 7, though a few larger centers have populations larger than can be supported by land within a two kilometer catchment and might therefore require tribute from their dependencies, there is no regular relation between size of settlement and estimated productivity of its immediate environment. In this case, the extensive soil and agronomic studies of the Susiana Plain and recent paleobotanical studies insure that our productivity estimates are relatively accurate. There are, however, two other possible reasons why the predicted relation does not exist. First, while our estimates of regional population, based on average housing densities, may be approximately correct, the estimate for a particular site at a particular time is difficult when housing density can vary for social reasons. Second, and perhaps more important, in Greater Mesopotamia, unlike Mesoamerica, only part of the subsistence resources were raised within the settlement's immediate catchment area. In particular, domestic animals

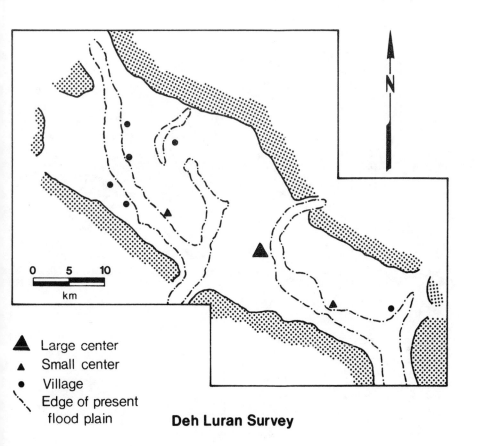

FIGURE 5

**Farukh Phase Settlements on the Deh Luran Plain**
(Source: Wright 1981:Fig. 32 and personal communication from James A. Neely)

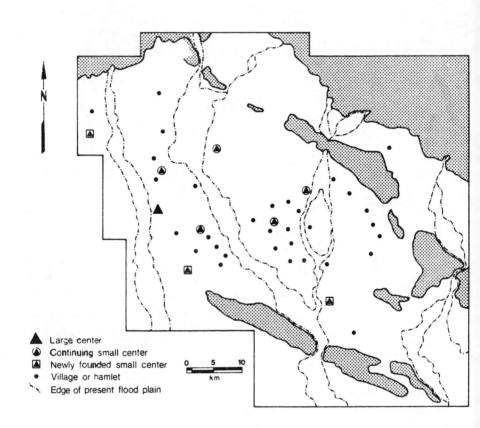

**FIGURE 6**

**Suse Phase Settlements on the Susiana Plain**

(Source: Survey Notes on file at the University of Michigan
Museum of Anthropology and personal communication from Frank Hole)

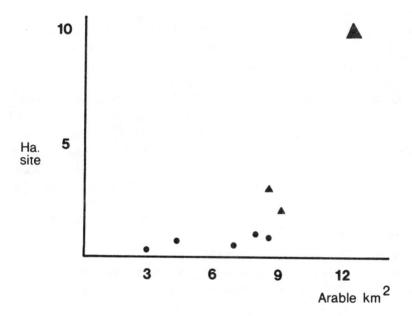

**FIGURE 7**

**The Relation between Site Size and Catchment Productivity
of Farukh Phase Sites on the Deh Luran Plain**

(Sources: Site size and Phase ascription are based on personal communication from
James A. Neely. "Arable kilometers squared" is irrigatable land within a two
kilometer radius, with land shared between adjacent sites divided between
them, derived from Neely's base map and Kirkby 1976)

would have been taken out to marginal pastures, perhaps in distant hilly regions. Since much tribute may have been extracted as animals and animal products, the productivity of a site's immediate environs may have had little to do with its tribute payments and its population size. Wherever domestic animals are so used, one can expect problems of this sort with site catchment studies.

Fortunately we have another form of evidence, the seal impressions, relevant to the mobilization of goods as tribute. From Susa during the Suse Phase, a useful sample of sealings as well as seals exist. If the samples are representative, the proportion of seals with complex motifs should be proportional to the numbers of politically important individuals at Susa, assuming similar rates of discarding the varieties of seals. The proportion of sealings with such motifs should be proportional to the relative number of acts of authorization which such individuals perform. Table 1 shows that only 8% of the Suse sealings are of the complex varieties; in contrast 50% of the admittedly small sample of sealings were made with complex varieties of seals. On present evidence, it

### TABLE 1
#### Seals and Seal Impressions from Suse Phase Susa
(Sources: Amiet 1972; Le Brun 1971)

|                      | SEALS | IMPRINTS |
|----------------------|-------|----------|
| Simple Designs       |       |          |
| Linear Geometric     | 92    | 8        |
| Animals              | 31    | 5        |
| Other                | 5     | —        |
| Complex Designs      |       |          |
| Master of Animals    | 2     | 3        |
| Cruciforms           | 6     | 7        |
| Other                | 2     | 3        |
| Total Simple         | 128   | 13       |
| Total Complex        | 10    | 13       |

seems that only a small proportion of the seal-holders were concerned with a majority of the transactions authorizing goods storage and transfer. More precise assessments of the control of goods must await the further recovery of sealings in well-defined contexts from subsidiary settlements as well as centers, and also the analysis of the types of containers being sealed (cf. Le Brun and Vallat 1978; Wright, Miller, and Redding 1980:277-281 for such studies on later periods).

The regulation of production economies is always necessary, if only because natural productivities and human populations vary from year to year. The demands of political paramounts further compound the difficulties of the agricultural decision-maker. Does the evidence of special craft products or exotic materials in southwestern Iran conform to that expected if the distribution of such items signaled effective political control of production? Some evidence is available from the Farukh Phase layers at the subsidiary center of Farukhabad on the Deh Luran Plain as noted above (Table 2 from Wright 1981:12-22, Appendix Tables A2, B1, D14). Refuse samples are associated with a sequence involving the final use and decay of an Early Farukh Phase elaborate residence, a time of no evident construction, construction of new buildings in the middle of the Middle Farukh Phase, and their use through the end of the Middle Farukh Phase. Other samples are associated with a sequence of approximately contemporary simple residences. These samples, as was the case from Oaxaca, were not collected with questions of tributary regulation in mind, and they are neither large enough nor sufficiently well-dated to evaluate definitively such questions. Nevertheless, in the absence of other data, their consideration is useful. The period of the use and decay of the first elaborate building saw moderate bitumen production, a local export-oriented activity (Wright 1981:268-270) and moderate use of redistributed imported cherts (Wright 1981:268). Just before the construction of the new elaborate building and its associated storage structures bitumen production increased—notably around the more elaborate buildings. These indications of greater production for export and greater consumption of

## TABLE 2
### Bitumen Waste and Chert Blade Occurrences at Tepe Farukahabad

| LAYERS SCREENED (M³) | EVENTS | BITUMEN WASTE/M³ | BLADES/BLADE SEGMENTS | | |
| --- | --- | --- | --- | --- | --- |
| | | | LOCAL CHERT/M³ | EXOTIC CHERT/M³ | % EXOTIC CHERT |
| **Excavation A: The Sequence of Elaborate Buildings** | | | | | |
| 24-25 (7.57) | Use | 7.5 | .5 | 1.1 | 67% |
| 26 (2.50) | | .7 | 3.6 | 3.2 | 47% |
| 27 (4.40) | Build | 5.4 | 1.8 | 3.6 | 66% |
| 28 (4.25) | Build? | 2.0 | 2.1 | .9 | 31% |
| 29 (12.00) | Decay | 4.1 | 1.7 | .5 | 23% |
| 30 (1.50) | Use | 27.9 | 4.0 | 1.3 | 25% |
| | Build | | | | |
| **Excavation B: The Sequence of Simple Buildings** | | | | | |
| 40 (3.77) | | 65.9 | 5.3 | 3.7 | 41% |
| 41 (6.20) | | 35.9 | 1.6 | 1.3 | 44% |
| 42 (4.50) | | 60.1 | 2.0 | .9 | 31% |
| 43 (6.00) | | 19.0 | 1.2 | .3 | 22% |
| 44 (4.10) | | 6.0 | 2.2 | 1.2 | 36% |
| 45 (3.60) | | 2.7 | 2.2 | 1.4 | 38% |
| 46 (3.80) | | 7.9 | 2.4 | 2.9 | 55% |

redistributed items continues throughout the period of use of this building. Unfortunately, refuse samples associated with the third elaborate building of the Late Farukh Phase, built on the wall stubs of the second without evidence of a period of decay, are too small to permit analysis. In general, throughout that part of the sequence for which this kind of detailed analysis can be attempted, bitumen production around the modest buildings correlates positively with exotic cherts around the more elaborate buildings (r=.98, n= 6; R@.01=.87). This pattern and the indication that the rebuilding of elaborate residences follows increases in local resource extraction and redistribution conform with the proposition that distribution regulates local production and political relations; however, they also conform with several other modelings of Late fifth millennium political economy. A critical test would require an articulation of the evidence of redistribution and production with evidence of conflict and political re-organization. Such evidence is not available from Farukhabad.

From the Susiana Plain during the same and later periods, evidence of both reorganization and conflict exists. In the first place, the group of larger centers in the middle of the Susiana Plain, dominant throughout the early and middle fifth millennium, were abandoned or became very small; and the plain became dominated by the newly founded major center of Susa. Foundation of a new center with a massive ritual focus in its central platform, probably indicates a new or newly re-sanctified paramount lineage. Unfortunately we do not know to what extent this spatial re-organization was related to internal conflict. Later, however, there is evidence of conflict at Susa (Perrot 1972; Canal 1978). The great platform replaced several smaller platforms. After a period of prosperity, the central structure was overthrown, with evidences of fire (Canal 1978: Fig. 7) and a body in the debris (Canal 1978:40-41; Fig. 10, pl. iv). After a period of neglect during the middle of the Suse Phase, the platform was restored; it continued in use until the Terminal Suse Phase when the elaborate painted pottery was ceasing to be made and other changes related to the final breakup and transformation of chiefly society were occurring. Unfortunately, this clear case of conflict, which would indicate some degree of political re-organization whether it resulted from external attack or internal rebellion, cannot yet be associated with evidence of possibly redistributed craft goods because the artifactual evidence from this most recent Suse Phase excavation has not yet been studied in detail.

In sum, the archaeological evidence in early southwestern Iran shows that the implications of the theoretical construct previously outlined appear reasonable. There are examples of symbols distinctive to the ranking class, used in a variety of situations critical to political-economic control. Subsidiary centers were located in positions better suited for tribute extraction than for the provisioning of goods and services to villages, and there are examples in which the rare seals with the more complex symbolism are used in a majority of the instances of the authorization of goods' movement and storage. In the long term, there are also examples of the overthrow of old centers. In the shorter term, there are examples of the fluctuation in chiefly display and redistribution correlated with the extraction of goods for export. Some features of the evidence, however, may not conform to the implications of the integrated construct. It is notable that the material evidence for a ranking class ideology exists only for the latest pre-state polity in southwestern Iran. On present evidence, the residential indications of class segregation and the settlement pattern features indicative of tribute extraction appeared in Deh Luran centuries earlier than the material correlates of the ideology that would justify support of such a political economy. However, present evidence is surely insufficient, and only excavation at some of the major centers older than Susa, using the precise artifact recovery and analysis techniques developed at Susa, Djaffarabad, and Farukhabad, can establish that this is an order of appearance contrary to the theoretical considerations presented earlier in this paper.

## Concluding Remarks

At the least, this review of some recent research in Mesopotamia and Mesoamerica shows that class-organized, socio-political organization flourished for centuries before actual state formation. Complex chiefdoms were not mere evolutionary curiosities, transformed immediately into states in the continental heartlands, persistent only on islands not large enough to sustain states. Also, I hope that the reader will see that it is indeed possible for archaeologists to answer questions about the formulation and uses of ideologies and the processes of political control. Beyond such substantive and methodological points, however, are other, perhaps more interesting, issues.

As an introduction to my argument, I suggested that continued competition for alliances and offices among local ranking groups would weld such groups into a region-wide chiefly or noble class, though I do not have the data to test such a developmental proposition, and I did not attempt to elaborate it. I have, however, tried to evaluate the proposition that (1) such a process of competition should generate an ideology of chiefly sanctity sufficient to command regular tribute from commoner producers, (2) that such an exaction of tribute should structure the hierarchy of chiefly centers, and (3) that the circulation of exotic materials and elaborate craft goods would help to control the proliferation of both nobles and commoners, the rate of extraction of tribute, and the disposition of offices by encouraging rebellion and warfare. Some of the evidence from southwestern Iran conforms with the implications of these proposals and some does not. Even if future research sustains these propositions, however, I suspect that a useful modeling of chiefdoms would require that additional propositions be constructed. Simulation using such an operational model under a variety of conditions would probably show that complex chiefdoms can be a resiliant kind of socio-political formation, a pattern that is reinstituted even after periods of political fragmentation and economic collapse.

If the implications of such simulations are verified by the

70 *Henry T. Wright*

evidence of archaeologically documented cases of cultural development, then the question of state origins becomes all the more challenging. States would not be a simple product of increases in scale, with consequent specializations in organization following a pragmatic logic. If complex chiefly formations have the capacity to reconstitute themselves after crisis and collapse, how are we to explain why they are, in some cases, reconstituted as states? I suggest that the answer may lie in the particular variant of the crisis situation, expressible in terms of variables describing the pattern of competition within and between polities, the assessments their leaders make of each other, the strategies they use, and so on. The development of such suggestions into a possible explanation of state origin, however, is best left for another paper.

## Acknowledgments

This paper would not have been possible without knowledge shared by those of my colleagues who work with the evidence of the fifth millennium settlements of southwestern Iran, particularly James Neely, Frank Hole, Kent Flannery, Geneviève Dollfus, and Alain Le Brun. It has profited from close readings and comments by Gregory Johnson and Susan Pollock. Joyce Marcus has corrected some of my misunderstandings of Formative Oaxaca. Timothy K. Earle has been an editor patient beyond measure. The reader will realize that this is a work in progress; the author takes full responsibilities for any shortcomings and requests that comments be sent to him care of the Museum of Anthropology in Ann Arbor, Michigan.

# References

Amiet, Pierre
1972   Glyptique Susienne. *Memoires de la Délégation Archéologique Française en Iran* No. XLIII. Paris: Guethner.

Benson, Elizabeth
1968   *Dumbarton Oaks Conference on the Olmec.* Cambridge, Mass.: Harvard University Press.

Bloch, Maurice
1977   The Discontinuity between Rank and Power as a Process. In *The Evolution of Social Systems,* edited by J. Friedman and M. J. Rowlands. London: Duckworth.

Brumfiel, Elizabeth
1976   Regional Growth in the Eastern Valley of Mexico: A Test of the "Population Pressure" Hypothesis. In *The early Mesoamerican village,* edited by K. Flannery. New York: Academic Press.

Canal, Denis
1978   La Terrasse haute de l'Acropole de Suse. *Cahiers de la Délégation Archéologique Française en Iran* 9:11-56.

Carniero, Robert
1981   The Chiefdom: Precursor of the State. In *The Transition to Statehood in the New World,* edited by Jones and Kautz. Cambridge: Cambridge University Press.

Dollfus, Geneviève
1971   Les fouilles à Djaffarabad de 1969 à 1971. *Cahiers de D.A.F.I.* 1:17-86.
1978   Djaffarabad, Djowi, Bendebal: Contribution à l'ètude de la Susiane au V$^e$ millénaire et au debut du IV millénaire. *Paleorient* 4:141-167.

Drennan, Robert D.
1976a    Religions and Social Evolution in Formative Mesoamerica. In *The early Mesoamerican village*, edited
by K. Flannery. New York: Academic Press.
1976b    Fábrica San José and Middle Formative Society in
the Valley of Oaxaca. *Memoirs of the Museum of
Anthropology* 8. Ann Arbor: University of Michigan, Museum of Anthropology.

Dyson, Robert H.
1966    *Excavations on the Acropolis of Susa and the Problems of Susa A, B, and C.* Unpublished Thesis in
Department of Anthropology. Cambridge: Harvard
University.

Earle, Timothy K.
1977    A reappraisal of redistribution: Complex Hawaiian
chiefdoms. In *Exchange Systems in prehistory*,
edited by T. Earle and J. Ericson, pp. 213-229. New
York: Academic Press.
1978    Economic and Social Organization of A Complex
Chiefdom: The Halelea District, Kauai, Hawaii.
*Anthropological Papers of the Museum of Anthro-
pology* 63. Ann Arbor: Museum of Anthropology.

Flannery, Kent V., Joyce Marcus, and Stephen A. Kowaleski
1981    The Preceramic and Formative of the Valley of
Oaxaca. In *Supplement to the Handbook of Middle
American Indians* I, edited by J. Sabloff. Austin:
University of Texas Press.

Flannery, Kent V., and Marcus Winter
1976    Analyzing Household Activities. In *The early Mesoamerican village*, edited by K. Flannery. New York:
Academic Press.

Frankenstein, Susan, and M. J. Rowlands
  1978    The internal structure and regional context of Early
          Iron Age society in Southwestern Germany. *Bulletin*
          15:73-112. London: Institute of Archaeology, Uni-
          versity of London.

Friedman, Jonathan
  1975    Tribes, States, and Transformations. In *Marxist
          Analyses in Social Anthropology*, edited by Bloch.
          *ASA Studies* 3 London: Association of Social An-
          thropology, Malaby Press Ltd.

Helbaek, Hans
  1969    Plant Collecting, Dry Farming, and Irrigation Agri-
          culture in Prehistoric Deh Luran. In *Prehistory and
          human ecology of the Deh Luran Plain*, edited by
          F. Hole, K. Flannery and J. Neely. Ann Arbor:
          University of Michigan, Museum of Anthropology.

Helms, Mary W.
  1979    *Ancient Panama: Chiefs in Search of Power*. Austin:
          University of Texas Press.

Hole, Frank
  1982    Unity and Autonomy: Prehistoric Society in Iranian
          Khuzistan. Unpublished paper Presented to the New
          York Academy of Sciences.

Hole, Frank, Kent V. Flannery, and James A. Neely
  1969    Prehistory and Human Ecology of the Deh Luran
          Plain. *Memoirs of the Museum of Anthropology* 1.
          Ann Arbor: University of Michigan, Museum of An-
          thropology.

Johnson, Gregory A.
  1982    Organizational Structure and Scalar Stress. In
          *Theory and Explanation in Archaeology*, edited by
          C. Renfrew, M. J. Rowlands, and B. A. Segraves.
          New York: Academic Press.

Kirkby, Michael J.
    1976    Land and Water Resources of the Deh Duran and
            Khuzistan Plains. In *Studies in the Archaeological
            History of the Deh Luran Plain: The Excavation of
            Chaga Sefid*, by F. Hole. *Memoirs of the Museum
            of Anthropology* 9. Ann Arbor: University of
            Michigan, Museum of Anthropology.

Kramer, Carol
    1980    Estimating Prehistoric Populations: an ethnoarchae-
            ological Approach. In L'Archéologie de L'Iraq du
            début de l'époque Néolithique à 333 avant notre
            ère, *Colloque Internationaux du Centre National
            de la Recherche Scientifique* 580. Paris: Editions
            du C.N.R.S.

Le Breton, Louis
    1957    The Early Periods at Susa. *Iraq* 19:79-114.

Leach, Edmund
    1954    *Political Systems of Highland Burma.* Cambridge:
            Cambridge University Press.

Le Brun, Alain
    1971    Recherches stratigraphiques a L'Acropole de Suse
            (1969-1971). *Cahiers de D.A.F.I.* 1:163-216.

Le Brun, Alain, and François Vallat
    1978    "L'origin de l'ecriture a Suse. *Cahiers de D.A.F.I.*
            8:11-59.

Marcus, Joyce
    1976    The Origins of Mesoamerican Writing. *Annual Re-
            view of Anthropology* 5:35-67.

Miller, Naomi
    1978    Preliminary Report on the botanical remains from
            Tepe Djaffarabad. *Cahiers de D.A.F.I.* 7:49-53.

    1981    The Plant Remains. In *An early town on the Deh
            Luran Plain*, edited by H. Wright. Ann Arbor: Uni-
            versity of Michigan, Museum of Anthropology.

Miroschedji, Pierre de
 1981    Le dieu Elamite au serpent et aux eaux jaillissantes. *Iranica Antiqua* XVI:1-25.

Morgan, Jaques de
 1912    Observations sur les couches profondes de l'Acropole de Suse. *Mémoires de la Délégation en Perse* XIII:1-25.

Peebles, C. S., and Susan M. Kus
 1977    Some Archaeological Correlates of Ranked Societies. *American Antiquity* 42:421-448.

Perrot, Jean
 1972    Travaux de la Mission de Suse depuis 1969. *Proceedings of the 1st Annual Symposium on Archaeological Research in Iran.* Teheran: Ministry of Culture and Arts, Iranian Centre for Archaeological Research.

Pollock, Susan
 1983    Style and Information: An Analysis of Susiana Ceramics. *The Journal of Anthropological Archaeology* (in press).

Pyne, Nanette M.
 1976    The Fire Serpent and Were-jaguar in Formative Oaxaca: A Contingency Table Analysis. In *The early Mesoamerican village*, edited by K. Flannery. New York: Academic Press.

Redding, Richard W.
 1981    The Faunal Remains. In *An early town on the Deh Luran Plain*, edited by H. Wright. Ann Arbor: University of Michigan, Museum of Anthropology.

Renfrew, Colin
 1973    Monuments, Mobilization and Social Organization in Neolithic Wessex. In *The Explanation of Culture Change: Models in Prehistory*, edited by Colin Renfrew. London: Duckworth.

Sahlins, Marshall
  1963    Poor Man, Rich Man, Big Man, Chief: Political
          Types in Melenesia and Polynesia. *Comparative
          Studies* in *Society and History* V:285-303.
  1977    The State of the Art in Social/Cultural Anthropol-
          ogy. In *Perspectives in Anthropology 1976. Special
          Publication of the American Anthropoogical Asso-
          ciation* 10. Washington, D.C.: American Anthro-
          pological Association.
  1981    *Historical Metaphors and Mythical Realities.* Ann
          Arbor: University of Michigan Press.

Service, Elman
  1962    *Primitive Social Organization* New York: Random
          House.

Steponaitas, Vincas
  1978    Location Theory and Complex Chiefdoms: A Missis-
          sippian Example. In *Mississippian Settlement
          Patterns*, edited by B. Smith. New York: Academic
          Press.
  1981    Settlement Hierarchies and Political Complexity in
          Nonmarket Societies: The Formative Period in the
          Valley of Mexico. *American Anthropologist* 83:
          320-363.

Stéve, M.-J., and H. Gasche
  1973    L'Acropole de Suse. *Mèmoires de la Dèlègation Ar-
          chèologique Française en Iran* XLVI Paris: Gueth-
          ner.

Winter, Marcus J., and Jane Wheeler Pires-Ferreira
  1976    Distribution of Obsidian Among Households in Two
          Oaxacan Villages. In *The early Mesoamerican vil-
          lage*, edited by K. Flannery. New York: Academic
          Press.

Wright, Henry T.
  1977    Recent Research on the Origin of the State. *Annual
          Review of Anthropology* 6:379-397.

Wright, Henry T., editor
  1981   An Early Town on the Deh Luran Plain: Excavations at Tepe Farukhabad. *Memoirs of the Museum of Anthropology* 13. Ann Arbor: University of Michigan, Museum of Anthropology.
Wright, Henry T., and Gregory A. Johnson
  1975   Population, Exchange and Early State Formation in Southwestern Iran. *American Anthropologist* 77:267-289.
Wright, Henry T., Naomi Miller, and Richard W. Redding
  1980   Time and Process in an Uruk Rural Community. In *Colloque Internationaux du Centre National de la Recherche Scientifique* 580. Paris: Editions du C.N.R.S.

# MESOPOTAMIAN SOCIAL EVOLUTION:
## OLD OUTLOOKS, NEW GOALS

Robert Mcc. Adams

The social sciences exist today in a condition of vague, fre-quently contentious, paradigmatic pluralism, what Clifford Geertz (1980) has characterized as "blurred genres." This is a description, not a criticism. Some level of contentiousness can hardly be avoided, since the growth of knowledge about society is always to some extent tied to the clash of conflicting ideas and even ideolo-gies. Moreover, we have learned from Thomas S. Kuhn (1970) that the natural course of scientific advance is neither continuous nor uni-directional. Phases of normal growth are accompanied by a progressive accumulation of anomalies unexplained by (if not contrary to) existing theories, until ultimately most investigators in a field turn rather abruptly toward a new theory and problem-atic. Little is to be gained from attempts at artificial or premature suppression of diversity. In most fields, and certainly in ours, new syntheses of even modest generality and power seem remote.

On the other hand, costs are associated with our prevailing pre-occupation with constituting and refining theoretical approaches that "pass like ships in the night." Implicit in this preoccupation is the attachment of higher value to advances in theory than to the detailed refinement, sifting and evaluation of evidence. However, the mutual isolation of the resultant strategies of investigation lowers the inducement to identify evidence that would be essential either for fitting them together in some new way or for choosing between them. An acceptance of such isolation as natural tends to convey the impression that proposed causal explanations need to be kept simple and intact, that they are somehow weakened by adulteration. But quite to the contrary, where progress has most notably been made toward what should be "just one science of men in time" (Bloch 1964:47) on the basis of adequate data, supposedly competing explanations usually have been found additive and interacting. What also seems clear is that explanation must advance hand in hand with explication if it is to be other than speculative. Edmund R. Leach may have irritated many archaeologists in telling them that "when the facts of history are known *in detail*, 'explanations' which are in any way adequate are always enormously complicated" (1973:769). But this is no less than an accurate summarization of the growing agreement about the multiplicity of factors involved—although not about their detailed order of primacy and modes of articulation—in a major historical transition like the one from feudalism to capitalism to which Leach was specifically referring (cf. Stone 1972; Brenner et al. 1977-78).

With regard to the origin and subsequent development of complex, civilized society in ancient Mesopotamia, there are two principal clusterings of approach that heretofore have maintained little communication with one another. One is prevailingly philological in orientation, while the other belongs in the research tradition of the social sciences. Both are comprised of a distinctive intertwining of underlying (often unstated) premises, strands of theory, priorities for investigation, accepted methods, and preferred bodies of data. Both have been effective in organizing the work of scholars and in generating fresh insights and questions. But there are limitations and lacunae in each that need to be recognized, both in order to build on potential combinations of their strengths and to facilitate new inquiries. Further advances in understanding Mesopotamian sociocultural evolution (surely a "pristine" as well as uniquely well-documented case with writing introduced toward the end of the fourth millennium) will depend on features drawn from both approaches.

## Orientations in Assyriology

Much the older and larger of the two approaches is firmly identified with the humanities. It includes a relatively small, for the
most part descriptively oriented group of archaeologists whose
excavations have provided the greater part of the data on which
the field relies. More crucial to my present theme is the Assyriological wing, even though its dominant orientations are philological and hermeneutic rather than synthetic and explanatory. That
is to say, its interest and strength lie less in a sense of societal
problem, process or context and more in mastery of the relevant
source materials, sensitivity to nuance, and fidelity to detail.

Most Assyriological writing tends to be limited by the world
view of its scribal informants. Concerns embodied in the texts
largely determine assumptions and priorities, while the scribes'
probable biases or oversights receive less attention. There is a preoccupation with the central state and religious organizations and
the social elites whom the scribes served, and only occasional
interest in the subordinate, largely agricultural population at or
beyond the peripheries of the scribal field of vision. Instructions
and codes of laws receive more stress than variations in how they
were received or responded to. Prevailingly philological priorities
lead to a concentration on selected examples of transactions or
narratives that are unusually well preserved or rich in detail, rather
than on quantitative analysis seeking to establish ranges of variance as well as norms. While particular ceremonies, institutions
and the like sometimes are described, little effort is devoted to
reconstructing the long and usually very incompletely documented
sequences of transactions linking, for example, production with
distribution and final consumption.

The scribal standpoint that Assyriology has adopted is distinct-
ively urban. It is also embedded in a literary tradition that was
committed to continuity. Relatively fleeting periods of political
integration and prosperity are highlighted during which textual
output was at its highest, rather than the longer and more frequent
periods of stagnation or breakup. Rare episodes of centralization

are used as a basis for models of holistic equilibrium, with little concern for how the disjunctions between such equilibria could have been bridged by transitional processes not recorded in the texts. Naturally there is a great deal of scholarly diversity that cannot be portrayed in general remarks like these, and numerous individual studies can be cited that run counter to my generalizations. Moreover, the proportion of the exceptional cases is increasing. But at least until recently and in the aggregate, these are the characteristics of the field whose primary textual analyses and translations alone can feed wider interests in synthesis, theory and comparison.

Many, perhaps even most, of the characterizations just given are not so much imposed by the field of scholarship as they are the ineluctable consequences of its source materials (Oppenheim 1964: chapter 1). Cuneiform archives tend to be incidental points of light in a vast, dark room. Accidents of discovery and preservation play a profound, if largely unacknowledged, part in the selection of fruitful problems and methods. The preoccupation with narrow questions of dynastic chronicle may have been more enthusiastic and protracted than was necessary, but in fairness was in good part indispensable if there was to be established a temporal and political context for more precessually oriented studies. Administrative records focus narrowly on particular relationships or transactions in what were once complex, extended series. While a Sumerian proverb recognizes that "The poor are the silent of the land" (Gordon 1959:196), account is otherwise almost never given of what went unrecorded and why. Serious efforts at interpretation, whether of latent motives, of alternatives considered and rejected, of perceived constraints on courses of action, or of sources of conflict, generally lay outside the scribal purview. The obvious could also be safely neglected, since it was already familiar to all those commissioning and using the texts. One authority has concluded pessimistically that the closer a cultural datum lay to the core of human activities of the time, the greater are the chances that no record was made of it (Civil 1980:228). And adequate numbers of substantially understood texts do not really antedate the mid-third millennium B.C., although by that time urban and in some senses literate civilization was already seven or eight centuries old. The origin of the state and civilization is a classic problem for anthropology, but almost by definition it lies largely outside the province of Assyriology.

A civilizational frame of reference is perhaps most consonant with an Assyriological approach. By this I refer to an orientation to a complex cultural tradition that is of large scale although rather indefinitely bounded in space and time, embracing a succession of cities and states and an aggregation of central as well as marginal peoples. As noted, Assyriologists tend to concentrate on the formal, upper levels of such a configuration.

Essentially the same frame of reference is necessary for most historical and anthropological studies. It is Mesopotamian civilization, rather than its component cities or states, to which Fernand Braudel's *longue durée* is applicable. Studies of technological, subsistence and environmental infrastructures assume a civilizational context. Within such a context a place can be found for rural as well as urban elements, horizontal relationships as well as hierarchical superstructures, and local as well as regional specialization, cooperation, and competition. While there is a risk of overemphasizing cohesiveness and uniformity, we tend to associate Mesopotamian civilization with a particular world-view. And both supporting and supported by this world-view were enduring structures of social relations that transcended localized clusterings in particular cities as well as ephemeral concentrations of power in particular dynastic states.

## Current Applications of Systems Theory

Systems theory is today the most actively and effectively pursued explanatory approach in anthropological archaeology. It should build upon the Assyriological tradition of mastery of textual sources, seeking to orient part of it toward more generalizing and comparative goals. As yet, however, only the beginnings of a trend in this direction can be discerned. And while the avoidance has been largely mutual, it may be worth noting that younger scholars with a predominantly humanistic background are now taking a more active interest in convergence than their counterparts in anthropological archaeology (e.g., Desrochers 1978; Kamp and Yoffee 1980; Larsen 1976; Marfoe 1980; Michalowski 1978; Robertson 1981; Stolper 1974; Yoffee 1981).

This can be explained in part by differences in orientation and training. The corpus of relevant Assyriological monographs or articles (not to speak of footnotes!), of interpretive tools such as dictionaries, and of translated cuneiform texts has been growing at an accelerating pace, and guides to the newly opened terrain that would make it intelligible to the social scientist are unavailable. (The same applies, of course, to the dearth of interpretive guides to recent social scientific work.) Mounting educational costs and employment uncertainties exert pressure to foreshorten graduate training, leaving less and less opportunity to explore unfamiliar fields. As archaeologists, those with a previously established interest in systems theory are generally most comfortable with the material, behavioral residues of pre- or non-literate cultures. Among those with a primarily anthropological orientation Mesopotamia, or even the whole of the ancient Near East, is a relatively minor regional specialization. The comparative outlook associated with anthropology as a discipline focuses attention on models generated in other, ethnographically familiar as well as archaeologically more intensively studied areas, rather than on a region where the primary tradition of scholarship is grounded on different premises.

Obviously most desirable would be the development of at least a small cadre of individuals with something approaching bivalence of competence. Yet how, and perhaps even whether, this can be attained is doubtful, at least if it is strictly defined in terms of the capacity to make fully independent judgments of comparable standard in both philology and anthropology. For one thing, breadth of familiarity with a wide temporal and geographic range of Assyriological sources tends to be of great importance even if one wishes to specialize only on a limited archive or genre. While basic command of the living language of one's fieldwork is regarded by most contemporary social anthropologists as a prerequisite, preparation to deal productively with the textual vestiges of a long evolving, imperfectly understood "dead" language is immensely more time consuming. Perhaps as a result, increasingly specialized, intra-disciplinary demands for graduate training have tended to take precedence. This discourages pursuit of even a more modest, intermediate objective, the development of critical awareness of the potentialities and modes of thought of another field of investigation. Significant as these deterrent factors are, however, the attenuated contacts also must reflect a mistaken order of priorities. It is of fundamental importance in advancing a *general* understanding of early civilizations for Mesopotamian archaeological and textual studies not merely to supplement one another but to interact synergistically. Why then has cross-fertilization been so limited, at least in the interchange of ideas if not of persons?

I think three basic features of the systems paradigm in anthropological archaeology have acted to inhibit interest in the immense resources of the Mesopotamian written record. One is a commitment to a behavioristic outlook that is simply too limited to do justice to documentary materials. The second is a willingness to accept as "scientific" only what takes place on archaeological and not historical time-scales. And third is an assumption that growth in social scale and complexity must be somewhat mechanically coupled to, and ultimately dependent on, a growing number of hierarchically specialized levels of administration. This is not the place for a full discussion of such general issues, but they must be dealt with at least briefly.

Lewis Binford has claimed that "behavior is the dynamics of adaptation" (1972:264) and archaeological behaviorism attaches central importance to adaptationist strategies. This has led to considerable advances in understanding when there is only archaeological evidence to consider, but is inadequate when textual evidence broadens our opportunities. Unless one is prepared to make the reductionist assumption that significant changes in behavior are exclusively due to a Darwinian selection, such changes cannot be fully understood without reference to the systems of meaning in which behavior is embedded. Similarly, in accounting for change, systems theorists have given primary attention to sketching feedback loops that would reinforce slow, not wholly purposive (if also not necessarily wholly unconscious) drifts into new routines. That may be the best, or even the only available, archaeological strategy, but as already noted it fundamentally distorts what we know of the way in which change occurs whenever there is adequate documentation.

Along the broadly overlapping border shared by archaeology and history, therefore, the archaeological systems approach needs to seek out indications of variable performance within decision units. Similarly, the tendency to demote historic outcomes to accidents—depersonalized, random concatenations of system variables and exogenous stresses—needs correcting. Neither of these things can be done without recognizing a hitherto ignored role for the expression of culturally prescribed forms of consciousness—pragmatic calculations of risk and cost, experimentation, alliance formation around partial convergences of interest, means-ends dilemmas, and the like.

The essential point is perhaps only a truism, but one well worth stating explicitly:

> From our own life, we feel that it is undeniable and true that human behavior is prominently shaped by consciousness and purpose. Anthropologists are therefore prepared to speak about things like beliefs, obligations, and values, not just immediate, overt behaviour. This also means that an explanatory model for behaviour can be different from the models used in natural science. (Barth 1966:20)

A corollary is that a considerable degree of autonomy must be allowed for among interacting levels, components, groups, and even individual actors. After all, the world generally consists of open, poorly articulated systems and loosely interacting sub-systems whose relationships to one another and to their environments are ambiguous and indecisive. As Jonathan Friedman has put it:

> An eco-system is not organized as such. It is the result of the mutual and usually partial adaptation of populations each of which has laws of functioning that are internally determined. It is the fact that the world is made up of relatively independent structures which must necessarily relate to one another in larger systems of reproduction . . . which is the root of variability, mutual limitation, and ultimately history. History is built on the failure of social forms as much as on their success. If social forms fail, it is because they have laws of their own whose purpose is other than making optimal use of their techno-environments. (1974:466)

Turning to time-scales, archaeologically based determinations alone can seldom fix particular finds, and still less the episodes or processes of change one would like to deduce from them, with a greater order of precision than ± 50 to 100 years. At least within present technical and budgetary constraints, therefore, four to eight generations is the minimal recognizable time unit in archaeology. But this is only a consequence of methodological limitations that archaeologists have had to live with for so long that they have come to take them for granted. Nothing dictates that the relatively slow pace of change perceptible through the use of such units is somehow more grounded in eco-systemic or structural realities than any other. Can we really detach a cultural system from "all the events, behaviors, or other transactional phenomena going on at a given time" and see it instead as "the conditioning framework within which all these events transpire," as Binford (1981:201) has recently argued? Or are historical societies both reproduced and transformed through their—always imperfect—instantiation in events? Fully recognizing the force of Braudel's observation that "the short-term is the most capricious and deceptive form of time" (1972:15), I would argue instead that

science lies as much in the unexpected, short-lived but illumin-
ating particular as in the abstract, long-term, and supposedly
retrodictable.

A further inhibiting feature in systems theory, I believe, is its
tendency to regard societal evolution as subsumed by the evolution of centralized, hierarchical coordination and control. That
hierarchies did grow is beyond question, as is the proposition that
they were frequently identified with regulatory functions. But
this is not to be equated with the social utility of such functions.
It is doubtful how far "higher-order regulators" materially contributed to the well-being and security of the societies that they
controlled. The plausible alternative explanation, at least in many
cases, is that elites were merely adept at finding ways to rationalize their imposition of arbitrary authority in pursuit of their own
self-interest (Gilman 1981).

Concepts like centralization, promotion, linearization and
hypercoherence (Flannery 1972) are useful additions to our
theoretical arsenal, but there is a risk that they will be employed
with reductionistic tidiness to suggest a kind of Malthusian growth
of hierarchies to or beyond the limits of tolerable stress for the
supporting society as a whole. This could lead to a neglect of the
importance of lateral, lower-level linkages of voluntary associa-
tions and interest groups, as well as the socially constitutive role
of entrepreneurship. Institutions generally have porous, changing
boundaries, and their personnel are continually faced with the
need to make situationally responsive choices on the basis of
conflicting commitments, statuses and loyalties. All this confusion
and uncertainty would quickly become evident if the models
were to be made responsive to textual as well as archaeological
data. But then they would lose the smoothness and consistency of
response to small-scale stress that has contributed to their popu-
larity among archaeologists in other regions lacking comparable
textual data. Hence the focus of systems theory remains on the
evolution of chiefdoms into pristine, initial states, safely anterior
to all but the earliest and least well understood of the texts. The
need for the dialogue remains, but it fails to develop.

Systems theorists have taken some steps toward overcoming these deficiencies by introducing "flows of information" as an emergent property that acquires additional importance with growing social scale and complexity. This at least gives formal recognition to the written nature of the primary data. But as yet, information has been treated only as an undifferentiated category, significant primarily for the gross amounts stored and circulated. The implication is that it had a centralizing, system-maintaining function, which by and large is certainly reasonable. But in fact, cuneiform writing had different roles in a variety of loosely integrated organizational and cognitive spheres. Hence there are many more steps to be taken as the unitary category "information" is analytically decomposed into the norm-inculcating, tradition-bearing, record-keeping, status- or power-asserting purposes that its scribal custodians were called upon to serve.

The complementarities and contrasts in the two approaches that I have sketched make apparent their combined potential in some suitably modified form. Each is particularly relevant for certain problems or levels of generality and not others; each values and concentrates on a largely distinctive body of data that the other can supplement; and each has limitations that the other can help overcome. My major concern in this paper is to illustrate how a prospective intersection and extension of them might enlarge the scope of our understanding.

## The Delineation of Shifting Sectoral and Institutional Boundaries

One prospective area of common concern and cooperation has already been implicit in earlier remarks. It seems more and more necessary to reject essentially all characterizations of monolithic or 'total' systems in antiquity. This applies, of course, to Karl Wittfogel's (1957) "hydraulic despotism." Urban civilization could not have arisen in a semi-arid region like Mesopotamia without irrigation. But the available data suggests that irrigation's effects on social institutions were quite circumscribed rather than pervasive. Since controls over irrigation were not preponderantly coercive or even bureaucratic, it is difficult to see how its managerial requirements could have given rise in any meaningful sense to cities, states, or a putatively despotic form of government. The all-embracing, unchecked and arbitrary exercise of power suggested by the term despotism distorts what was instead a shifting political struggle over people, resources, and security (Adams 1981, 1982a).

But Oriental despotism is only one of several assertions of totality, others of which serve us almost equally badly. The so-called temple economy of the early and mid-third millennium B.C. (cf. most recently Falkenstein 1954) is a case in point, now sufficiently well understood as one of a number of coexisting forms of social organization and land tenure so that a lengthy criticism of earlier claims for its inclusivity is no longer necessary. The same applies to the alleged state economy under the strongly bureaucratic Third Dynasty of Ur at the end of the third millennium. It has often been viewed in equally all-embracing terms, accentuating the relative abruptness of the transitions leading to and following this period. I. J. Gelb (1969:147-149) has persuasively argued against a conclusion that depends largely on the *argumentum ex silentio* that contracts dealing with land-sales have not been found; whether or not there were restrictions at the time on sales, he is able to affirm the existence of private holdings by numerous other kinds of testimony. However, my point is not simply that private and communal holdings in land and other forms of wealth existed alongside of state and temple holdings. Instead, as Gelb and Kazuya Maekawa (1973-74) have argued, we must recognize the persistence of different organizational principles and forms, even though they received different emphasis in different periods and localities. It is the fluctuating, plural pattern of their interaction over long periods that should become a primary focus of attention in our efforts at synthesis.

This argument perhaps should be re-cast in terms more generally intelligible to anthropologists. A generation ago it was widely assumed that the state and temple economies were largely

coterminous and virtually all embracing. Achieving wide circulation at   the time was Karl Polanyi's forceful articulation of a
"substantivist" (rather than "formal") analytic approach to the
political economies of archaic states. It was his position that these
were in general organized according to redistributive rather than
market principles, and a central part of his case was that "Babylonia, as a matter of fact, possessed neither market places nor a
functioning market system of any description" (Polanyi 1957:16).
While this apodictic form of his argument was generally ignored by
Near Eastern specialists, a qualified and more securely grounded
version of it by A. Leo Oppenheim (1957, 1964: chapter 2)
achieved wide influence among Assyriologists.

Since then, however, Mesopotamian and Near Eastern specialists
have increasingly challenged the application of a model of redistribution whose empirical support derives mainly from work on
chiefdoms and not on complex civilizations. Reliance on a single
rubric like redistribution, for example, tends to ignore crucial
differences with regard to ownership of the means of production.
Community members, cultivating their own lands with their own
implements, typically were the principal agency involved in production for chiefly storehouses. In Mesopotamia, on the other
hand, most of what was involved in redistribution were the products of corvée and dependent labor using state-supplied plows
and draft animals on lands directly held by the central authority.
It distorts their essential character to liken systems of this kind
to redistribution in chiefdoms. They are more accurately understood as "corporate systems fulfilling redistributive functions"
(Robertson 1981:31-33).

Considerable evidence meanwhile has accumulated for the existence of a vigorous entrepreneurial sector—risk-taking individuals
who speculated on price, calculated rates of profit, and manipu-
lated terms of exchange on their own behalf rather than as institutional agents. Citing the work of Gelb, Igor Diakonoff, K. R.
Veenhof and others, a recent review concludes that "the redistributive system that characterized [palace and temple estates] *did
not operate to the exclusion of* other sectors within the total

economic framework" and that "Polanyi's characterization of the Mesopotamian economy as almost exclusively redistributive and lacking any elements of a market system can no longer be supported" (Robertson 1981:29-30; italics original). And for market-places as well as markets, Polanyi's rejection of their existence "simply does not stand up to closer scrutiny" (Gledhill and Larsen 1982:203; cf. Muhly 1980:74; Yoffee 1981). It is vital to recognize instead the *coexistence* of what Oppenheim aptly termed the redistributive "great organizations" and a commercially oriented sector he identified with "the city" (Oppenheim 1964:95). Each had its associated modes of action, relationship, and belief, even though some of the same individuals may have simultaneously played substantial roles in both of them. Alongside of the voluminously recorded ration system that apparently governed the allocation of basic staples were other, almost unrecorded patterns of circulation applying to important commodities like pottery and fish. Surely these were primarily the products of specialists, working within an efficient and substantial, if perhaps discontinuous and on the whole informally organized, sphere of peddling and marketing activity that supplemented the redistributive apparatus.

Reaching the same evaluation, Marvin Powell has pointed out that the "overwhelming majority of all third-millennium records derive from the archives of great estates associated with the temple or central government," and that "these are internal records which concern themselves with what takes place outside only insofar as it directly concerns the expenditure and income of the state itself" (1977:25). This results in a skewing or foreshortening of view that is obviously difficult to overcome within the limitations of the same textual genres, but occasionally there are opportunities to do so. Powell finds it noteworthy, for example, that the Sumerian proverb literature has little to say about the temple and state bureaucracies. And the importance of a different, if poorly attested, outer world is also suggested by the fact that the social values expressed in the proverbs "clash with the assumption of a centrally organized economy in which each member of society, including the merchant, was essentially an employee of the central controlling authority" (Powell 1977:24-25).

This emergent consensus is both limited and tentative, and no doubt debate will continue on whether the presence of marketing elements fundamentally alters the Polanyi reconstruction or merely restricts its application (cf. Renger, in press). But a more concise restatement of the "pluralist" case may help to clarify the position taken here. Apart from the personnel closely identified with the "great organizations" of state and temple, there appears to have been a significant group of individuals, perhaps to be thought of as constituting a class, who conducted essentially private ventures for profit. As such, they were engaged in the accumulation of alienable forms of wealth that were capable of abstraction and could be large, and they self-consciously deployed their resources toward diverse ends. While privately held wealth did not function as directly in the production process as industrial capital does in our own times, some entrepreneurial attitudes and practices were similar to those associated with modern capitalism (Veenhof 1972; Larsen 1976). This does not mean that we can transfer directly to ancient society the full set of conceptions and terms that were developed for an entirely different institutional complex as the ancient economic system was fundamentally less self-generating and accumulative. But it seems equally inappropriate to deny or neglect the resemblances altogether, and simply to dismiss the possibility that modern economic concepts and methods can shed light on the ancient world as well.

We should not exaggerate the scale of the entrepreneurial sector or freedom of its action, for both were certainly restricted. A much larger part in the circulation of commodities probably was played, at least until well into the second millennium, by redistributive than by exchange processes. But capital loans for interest and profit-making ventures involving fishing rights and herding responsibilities all can be traced as far back as the late Early Dynastic period (Powell 1977:28). By no later than the Akkadian period the term *dam-gàr* referred to "a business agent who sought profits in cash or commodities for his clients" (Foster

1977:34) (among whom were, on some occasions, the palace and temple), as contrasted with other traders who concentrated on purchasing commodities to meet the state's requirements. So the roots of commercial entrepreneurship also reach far back in time, rather than merely florescing in the second millennium after earlier redistributive economies had run their course. And the earlier difference between the two unequal but coexisting sectors was substantial:

> The basic premise underlying the conception of the merchant presented here is that the merchant operated *primarily* on the basis of profit and loss and that the state or temple *never* undertook systematically to underwrite his losses. The evidence for this, like the evidence for everything else in the third millennium is disparate, uneven, and indirect, but, on the whole, it is far more compelling than the evidence which can be brought forward to support the view that profit was not an important motive in merchant activity. At the same time, it cannot be too strongly emphasized that 'important motive' does not imply 'sole motive', because we are often unable to determine the motives in contemporary economic activity, not to speak of ancient or medieval times. (Powell 1977:24)

Apart from the corporate and commercial sectors, there is still a third sphere of economic activity to be taken into account. Diakonoff (1972:48) was perhaps the first to recognize the existence of family communes and other types of corporate agricultural communities in records of land sales of the early third millennium, but regards them as a phase of unilineal evolutionary development that was permanently superseded. I (Adams, 1982b) have elsewhere taken issue with this unilinear view, arguing that suggestively similar organizational forms recur in later periods, and indeed, have maintained their importance on the rural scene until virtually the present day. If this is correct, there was a substantial social segment, perhaps even a great majority in many periods, that ventured outside the scope of a subsistence economy only to a limited extent.

There were, in short, fundamental cleavages within a society that too frequently has been described in unified, ideal-typical terms simply as "Mesopotamian." An immediate effect of identifying distinctive sub-patterns like these is to require that, insofar as possible, statements based on textual references be at least provisionally attributed to one or another sphere before larger patterns are asserted. Always most difficult to establish from the written sources will be the behavior, to say nothing of the motivations, of the agrarian population. Perhaps the major initiative in this respect must eventually be taken by the archaeologist, since at least the material residues of outlying peasant settlements should be fairly simple to recover. However, the theoretical treatment of a large, subsistence-oriented component of a complex society that I find most penetrating is an historically based study of a late feudal economy in eastern Europe (Kula 1976). Kula recognizes, as surely we must for the Mesopotamian case, that in dealing with serfs or more or less corporately organized peasant communities, the bisectoral nature of economic activity is fundamental. "Market phenomena (beginning with "pricing") affect only a small percentage of national production and consumption— i.e., that portion which passes through the market" (Kula 1976: 1974). Kula's primary concern is how to obtain a measure of what does not acquire a social estimation of value through market processes, and to plot through time the changing proportions of the market and non-market sectors. This problem of a moving interface between the two—further compounded by the redistributive activities of the great estates—greatly increases our difficulties. No sector's independence, dominance, or even systematicity can be taken for granted at any time.

If we are to work out the extent of governance of market pricing principles, the breadth and depth of the penetration of silver as a medium of exchange becomes a primary axis of investigation. As early as the Akkadian period silver was already in use for loans, deposits, purchases, rental payments, and as a standard of value for purposes of commercial record-keeping. It thus "may be considered money in the usual sense of that word" (Foster 1977:

35-36; see Powell 1978; Lambert 1963). There are suggestions that, by no later than the beginning of the second millennium, small quantities of silver might normally be at the disposition of even ordinary peasant households (Snell 1982:186). But barley also functioned as a parallel medium of exchange until well into the second millennium, permitting the subsistence-oriented population to rely largely on in-kind payments. What is of crucial importance is the extent to which payments of debts and taxes became monetarized.

> To the extent that this occurs, there is what could be called an 'obligation' to commercialize.' The peasant [or the peasant commune, or corporate group] is compelled to sell in order to obtain the money he needs to meet these financial obligations and not lose his plot. His reaction to the incentives of the market is diametrically opposed to what bourgeois economic science would expect: if prices go up, he sells less, and if they go down he has to sell more. The fiscal burden to which he is subject are basically fixed; therefore the amount sold (often at the expense of what is available for his own personal consumption) is inversely proportional to the price level. (Kula 1976:43)

Even the most voluminous historical records will seldom provide more than fragmentary clues to such patterns. Those in the ancient world who were involved in basic agricultural production were seldom if ever literate, and references to them by others tend to be concerned with degrees of compliance with delivery schedules rather than with demarcating a partly autonomous realm of peasant decision making. In trying to conceptualize the linkages between the peasant, administrative and entrepreneurial spheres, therefore, we may have to depend to an uncomfortable degree on what can be learned from modern dual economies in which cognitive as well as behavioral aspects are open for study. Direct testimony as to peasant beliefs and motivations likely will elude Assyriologists, and the prospect of archaeology filling the gap is not encouraging. While needing to remain sensitive to the issues in the old substantive/formalist quandary, we cannot afford to be deterred by it. As Norman Yoffee writes, "economic forces exist within social matrices, and the object is to get on with investigating the underlying factors of supply and demand as well as the institutional constraints upon their operation" (1981:5).

## Intersections of Demographic Change with Economic Supply and Demand

A second prospect for linking methods and paradigms that presently are largely isolated from one another is directly concerned with the factors of supply and demand and how they changed over time. One avenue of approach grows out of my recent synthesis of changing archaeological settlement and agricultural patterns (Adams 1981). Admittedly there is some tension between imprecise but fairly systematically acquired settlement pattern data and the specificity but lack of clear pattern or systematic coverage in the cuneiform texts. Settlement pattern data direct our attention toward broad generalizations about lengthy, not clearly demarked periods. Textual data only sporadically provide substantiation of, or contradictions to, such patterns. Yet we cannot proceed very far by keeping separate the archaeological and the textual data. To be made mutually relevant, they must be brought within a single interpretive context.

To illustrate one way of doing so, consider this overview of population and settlement trends on the central portion of the lower Mesopotamian plain (Table 1).

I will readily concede that there are problems in generalizing from these data. The proportionality of occupied site area to population is demonstrably not constant when dealing with individual settlements, and even as an average may have varied somewhat from period to period. Moreover, more intensive modern land use has precluded collecting comparable data for the northern part of the plain. This region includes Babylon and its hinterlands, where settlement trends in the second millennium may have partly

**TABLE 1**
Proportions of Urban and Rural Settlement
on the Lower Mesopotamian Plain
Fourth through Second Millennia B.C.
(after Adams 1981, Tables 7, 12 and 13)

| TIME | ARCHAEOL. PERIOD | OCCUPIED AREA IN HECTARES | PERCENT NON-URBAN (≤ 10 HECTARES) | PERCENT URBAN (≤ 40 HECTARES) |
|---|---|---|---|---|
| 4000 B.C. | | | | |
| | Early Uruk | 535 | 54 | 31 |
| | Late Uruk (Jemdet Nasr) | 583 | 50 | 24 |
| 3000 B.C. | | | | |
| | Early Dynastic I II | 1065 | 21 | 57 |
| | Early Dynastic III | 1659 | 10 | 78 |
| | Akkadian | 1416 | 18 | 63 |
| 2000 B.C. | Third Dynasty of Ur Isin-Larsa | 2725 | 25 | 55 |
| | Old Babylonian | 1791 | 30 | 50 |
| | Cassite | 1308 | 57 | 30 |
| | Middle Babylonian | 616 | 64 | 16 |
| 1000 B.C. | | | | |

compensated for the steep drop in population elsewhere. But the general direction and magnitude of the changes suggested by these figures is consistent in all regions that have been surveyed. It therefore seems reasonable to conclude that there was a long-term cycle of population growth and decline of major proportions.

Few would argue that there is a fixed relationship between population size and other economic variables. But just as surely the supply of productive resources was not completely elastic as the population expanded and contracted by a factor that may well have exceeded four times. So the finding in archaeological data of striking secular changes in demographic levels invites attention to textual data bearing on secular changes in the economy that may be in some way related to them. It would be premature to suggest an explanation for the cycle of growth and decline, and the Mesopotamian data alone are quite insufficient to indicate whether population is better treated as a dependent or an independent variable. But that there was *some* relationship between the changes that occurred and the standard of living, the relative prices of factors of production, and so on, seems self evident.

Even if this turns out not to be the case, or to be the case in some periods and not others, pursuit of the question is likely to be productive. Consider, for example, the price inflations that seem to have occurred in times of political breakdown, such as at the end of the Akkadian period under Sarkalisarri (I. J. Gelb, personal communication), perhaps already somewhat earlier during the reign of Naram-Sin (Kramer 1969:649), and again at the end of the Third Dynasty of Ur under Ibbi-Sin (Jacobsen 1953). By looking at these as dynamic processes, we may be able to plot the changing relationships and respective importance of the different socio-economic sectors mentioned previously. Consideration of supply and demand factors within a framework of changing population levels also may illuminate the effectiveness of the state apparatus in controlling economic oscillations, as both a manifestation of and contribution to its own power and stability.

There has been a sustained but limited interest among Assyriologists in price equivalences. Problems of geographic and temporal variations in units of measurement have often been regarded as almost insurmountable, and indeed, may prove to be so as additional data accumulates. In an essentially programmatic paper like the present one, however, I am deliberately setting aside such technical deterrents in order to discuss instead the broader theoretical context within which price variability may be especially meaningful. At least at this juncture, population trends give the best available set of clues to such a context.

Admittedly oversimplifying, the problem can be formalized in economic terms as a two-factor production function. The operational variable is the supply of labor, presumably closely dependent on changing overall population levels. The other major factor of production might at first glance appear to be land. Land is indeed a variable as a result of changing conditions with respect to soil quality, susceptibility to soil salinization, and ease of irrigation. McGuire Gibson (1974) has argued that there may have been violations of the alternate-fallow cycle as a result of overpopulation in certain districts at around the end of the third millennium, which would suggest land scarcity at least at that time. I think this implication is rendered somewhat doubtful, however, by the prevailingly low and relatively static sowing rates. If so, the more critical limits to agricultural production instead were set by in-season availability of irrigation water, which was always uncertain and never approached adequacy for the entire alluvial land surface. Thus the other factor of production involves some combination of land, capital, and water—mainly the latter. Perhaps it might be expressed as investment in irrigation flow stabilization and enhancement, which at the same time would improve waterborne transport.

An important theme for future, systematic investigation involves the price of labor relative to the price of land. Many factors are involved, so that no simple correlation is to be expected. First, there is very wide variation in the price of land. Even controlling to some extent for such variables as approximate contemporaneity, medium of payment, geographic sub-region, and access to water, sales are recorded at rates varying from ten to 200 sar per shekel of silver (Jakobson 1971:36). Vladimir Jakobson argues from these data that the "sale of land seems in most cases not to have been a completely voluntary act, but nearly always the result of economic pressure (or even of political pressure . . . )" 1971: 35), a conclusion which, while not unreasonable, applies, if in varying degrees, in every social system including our own. Particularly when our ignorance of the differential occurrence of deleterious conditions like soil salinization means that we are unable to assure ourselves that what is conveyed at grossly different prices are "essentially" identical plots of land," as Jakobson maintains, his conclusion seems unjustifiably sweeping that "no general concept of price for land had developed" (1971:37).

Howard Farber's (1978:26-30) data for northern Babylonia, based mainly on Sippar, suggest a progressive decline in both the sale and rental cost of land from around the time of Hammurabi until the end of the First Dynasty of Babylon in the latter part of the 17th century B.C. He attributes this to a decline in land productivity such as might be expected to result from soil salinization, and there is indeed independent evidence that salinization was a considerable factor in an ongoing reduction of crop yields during approximately the same period (Jacobsen and Adams 1958). But Farber also shows that, while the price of barley rose during this interval (consistent with a decline in land productivity), wages, whether paid in barley or in silver, increased somewhat more. This suggests either a gain in labor productivity so profound that it overcame the effects of increasing soil salinity, or else—and more likely—that increasing scarcity of labor drove up the relative cost of this factor of production.

This only begins to suggest the complexity of the factors that are involved. Farber provides a plausible response to earlier pessimistic judgments (Sweet 1957) that we would be unable to control for price inflation or deflation as a result of changing aggregate supplies of silver, showing that at least the sharper, short-term fluctuations affected only gold (Farber 1978:4-7). But secular trends in silver supply are still a possibility, and would have had their greatest effect precisely on the long-term relative movement of factor prices that would be most revealing as an indicator of economic trends. He also documents high-amplitude oscillations in the price of slaves, perhaps dropping to a low as a result of the extensive conquests of Hammurabi but then later undergoing a five-fold rise. Although slaves and wage-laborers were not interchangeable (a theme to which we shall return presently), surely this must have had some effect on the level of wages. State intervention also plays a part. Farber argues that in Old Babylonian times the palace "exercised a virtual monopoly on wool production" (1978:26), and in this way was able to stabilize wool prices. Yet even for the earlier, supposedly more statist Ur III period, Snell has shown that wool varied between 15 and 20 se (grains) of silver per mana (roughly, pound), that dates varied between 0.3 and 0.6 se per sila (roughly, quart), and that there were variations also in such staples as onions and fish. "The only reasonable way to interpret these facts," he continues, "is with the aid of formal, as opposed to Polanyi's substantivist, economic theory, namely that there were bad years and good years for onions and that individual producers made pricing decisions in reponse to forces we cannot now perceive" (Snell 1982: 191).

This changing relationship of costs for factors of production that are in relatively short or over-supply has been well documented for medieval and early modern Europe (e.g., Le Roi Ladurie 1974; Hilton 1975; Postan 1975; Cipolla 1980). How far it will be possible to do the same for ancient Mesopotamia is still problematical. While the prospect is attractive, only with a sustained effort is there a reasonable likelihood of success in demonstrating patterns in the fragmentary data. Much thought needs to be given to the possibility of alternative paths of analysis that can be employed if the most direct and obvious ones do not prove practicable. For example, attestations of amounts paid for labor and price equivalences may be too scattered in space and time to plot relationships over more than brief periods. Hired labor, in particular, is "seldom encountered" in texts of the Akkadian period (Foster 1977:38). Even by the Old Babylonian period, when it had become common (Klengel 1971:51), the several-fold disparity between daily and yearly rates (Farber 1978:33) suggests that the wage side of price/wage ratios involves many imponderables. But surely the size of ration allotments, which are common in the earlier periods, also was at least slowly and partially responsive to supply and demand factors. If so, perhaps it can be employed as a means of checking or amplifying price-wage comparisons, while also extending them backward in time. Similarly, in seeking to work out scales of remuneration it may prove helpful to determine equivalence in silver but in composite units of consumable goods. Then, even if absolute levels of consumption remain elusive at many points, insight into trends in the standard of living may be possible. Engel's law stipulates that as incomes rise the proportion of income spent on food, and *ceteris paribus* on low-income staples as opposed to fats and proteins, tends to decrease. Changes in the composition of a so-called 'market basket' of consumables, or perhaps even in normatively stated preferences, thus may provide clues to something more than inexplicable shifts in popular tastes.

To judge from the work of economic and demographic historians concerned with early modern Europe, there is every reason to expect that the large secular changes in population outlined earlier would have had widely ramifying effects. Much depends, of course, on whether or not the shifts occurred at rates sufficiently slow to permit orderly adjustment to them. The relatively sudden, heavy mortality associated with the Black Death in Europe (and the Near East) is well known, but the sustained population increases at rates exceeding one percent per annum that Le Roi Ladurie (1974) reports for Languedoc in the 16th century were in some ways equally catastrophic in their impact. Unfortunately, we can as yet say practically nothing about the rate at which population changes occurred in the ancient Near East. The survey data that have highlighted their existence offer little or no possibility of providing such information with any useful level of precision or reliability. But the question is obviously an important one calling for new, innovative lines of investigation, since many crucial processual questions hinge on being able to stipulate the approximate rate at which the change occurred.

Assuming relatively abrupt population shifts that appear to be documented archaeologically for Mesopotamia (Table 1), medieval and early modern European materials may provide suggestions as to what to look for in the textual sources. Pronounced population losses, such as those occurring from the Old Babylonian period onward, probably would have led to an inelastic, low demand for cereals and a shift of resources toward proportionately created consumption of meat and dairy products. Production of processed or manufactured commodities like metal utensils and textiles probably would not have declined as far or as rapidly as population levels, at least if English trends after the Black Death do not mislead us. Either this or improvements in technology and the supply of raw materials may be involved in what Snell characterizes as a "millennia long decrease in the price of copper" (1982: 203). High mortality and a sharply reduced population on occasion can be accompanied, in other words, by a relatively higher standard of living on the part of the surviving population. And one may anticipate that, under conditions of growing labor scarcity, elites and administrators would have sought to bind their labor force more closely by extending requirements for in-kind deliveries and involuntary services. For the peasantry, on the other hand, there were corresponding advantages in seeking contracted or paid labor instead—or in escaping fixed obligations through flight.

The long (if almost certainly irregular) rise in population from the late fourth through much of the third millennium in Mesopotamia (Table 1) is likely to have been associated with conditions that were in some respects the reciprocal of those just described. There may have been increases in technologically based productivity over this lengthy interval. This is strongly suggested by the apparent substitution of metal for clay and stone harvesting implements (Adams 1981:121); by the introduction of an extensive and well organized riverine transport system (Sauren 1966: passim); by the complexity of the centrally managed plowing present already in mid-third millennium Shuruppak (Lambert 1953:203); and by the introduction by about the same time of technical terms associated with increasingly specialized irrigation facilities (Nissen 1976:23). Possibly the spread of these innovations was enough to offset, or even more than offset, the threat to productivity from increasing salinization as the expanding agricultural perimeter led to greater reliance on lower back-slopes of levees and even on depressions with no external drainage. As total water withdrawals for irrigation increased to meet the needs of a growing population, however, the uncertainties of the Euphrates as a water source also would have represented an increasing threat to average agricultural productivity. Thus it is not unlikely that net productivity underwent a decline, and with it per capita income. If so, Engel's law predicts a shift toward lower quality dietary staples. Falling real income in relation to the value of foodstuffs and other commodities would have improved the bargaining position of those with large estates or administratively enforced labor requirements, while restricting the consumption of craft products not immediately needed for subsistence by the mass of the population. Reserves for contingencies such as a succession of bad harvests would have been eroded, leading to increasing burdens of debt on the agricultural sector of society and probably to the extension of stratification from the major urban centers into the smaller towns and even villages.

For ancient Mesopotamia, all of these suggestions can be put forward at present only quite speculatively. They embody a fairly straightforward, neo-classical projection of economic supply and demand factors that include population. As noted, such a projection finds empirical support in the relatively much richer and better understood data of medieval and early modern Europe. While this obviously does not assure its applicability to pre-industrial economies and societies more generally, it does provide suggestive and often surprising hypotheses to keep in mind as research on the ancient Near East moves forward.

Particularly fruitful in this respect are the contributions of the Cambridge Group for the History of Population and Social Structure, many of them recently summarized in a major work on "The Population History of England, 1541-1871" (Wrigley and Schofield 1981). One is "the striking absence of evidence that changes in real wages exert any considerable influence upon either short- or long-term national mortality fluctuations" (Wrigley and Schofield 1981:483). Mortality (i.e., changing life expectancy) may have been the most significant determinant of the magnitude of population swings, but its sources were unexpectedly exogenous to the economic system, and indeed, only fluctuated within a comparatively modest range. On the other hand, effects in the opposite direction were substantial. Deviations in rate of population increase or decrease beyond the half-percent or so to which English society apparently could accommodate led to much wider swings (in percentage terms) in price/wage ratios, in rents, and in agricultural/industrial output as well as price ratios. Given the substantial secular changes in population that archaeological surveys suggest took place in early Mesopotamia, it is reasonable to suppose that some economic changes may have taken place that were comparable to these.

A second important finding of the Cambridge Group concerns the role of fertility. As mortality was a positive check on population size, this was a major, independently acting preventive check. "It can be shown that changes in the timing and incidence of marriage in pre-industrial western Europe were large enough to offset the changes in mortality level commonly experienced" (Wrigley and Schofield 1981:461). But unlike the case with mortality, "on present evidence it appears highly likely that fertility did fluctuate in sympathy with prior changes in real wages, and that there was a long (approximately two-generation) lag between them" (Wrigley and Schofield 1981:461). While mortality must be viewed as predominantly an exogenous source of change, fertility, operating primarily through culturally prescribed prerequisites for marriage (access to land, status, relative age of spouses, etc.) was essentially an endogenous factor. And at least the English data indicate that, long before the Industrial Revolution, fertility was sometimes much less invariant than had been supposed. Marriage and birth-rates responded rapidly, in fact, to short-run variations in real wages as well as in death rates (Wrigley and Schofield 1981:354).

To be sure, the implications of these findings for the different cultural and historical context of early Mesopotamia must be regarded as hypothetical. The importance of fertility as a preventive check may rest largely on two specifically English complexes of belief and behavior that seem to have governed marriage decision during the early modern period: "the requirement of economic independence and the preference for nuclear households headed by a single married couple" (Wrigley and Schofield 1981: 354). If we remove or even reverse these cultural premises, the outcome would undoubtedly be very different. Then too, a monthly breakdown of mortality indicates wide variations by latitude. Winter and spring death-rates were regularly fifty percent higher in England and northern Europe, while in Mediterranean lands the summer was the deadly season. This argues for respiratory infections as the major cause of death in northern Europe, but for intestinal diseases in regions climatically more comparable to Mesopotamia (Wrigley and Schofield 1981:293-298). It is at least plausible that living standards exercised a greater influence on mortality resulting from intestinal than from respiratory diseases. Furthermore, even in the English data the available time-series for real wages are recognized as being incomplete and not wholly representative, especially with reference to discrepancies between individual wage rates and annual totals of family income. Shifts in patterns of consumption require shifts in the assumed contents of the market basket of consumables that is used to calculate real wages, placing further obstacles in the path of a comparison of aggregate living standards from period to period.

However, it must be borne in mind that the intent is not to impose the early English patterns on a recalcitrant historical sequence to which they manifestly do not apply. Instead, it is enough to see in the English case a stimulus to the construction and testing of more appropriate models. And we should recognize the possibility that archaeology can assist in this process by providing direct indices of living standards even if we remain poorly informed by texts as to changing real wages. Examples include the measurement of house-floor areas, skeletal stature, and protein intake from carbon and nitrogen isotope ratios in bone collagen (Anonymous 1982) or from strontium-calcium ratios in bone (Schoeninger 1981).

The objective of this effort is not simply to add another chapter to world demographic history, valuable as this might be in its own right. Instead, what is of primary interest are the intersections of demographic factors with other social and economic variables. These intersections reinforce broad contrasts in the qualities of life, in ways that the English data highlight. On the one hand, it became apparent to Malthus, and still seems applicable to many less-developed countries,

> that there was a pattern in pre-industrial demography arising from its basic characteristics. Fertility was high, and mortality could not be other than high also, its high level being maintained not by matching fertility year in year out but by intermittent, savage mortality spasms which pruned the population back sharply. In most years, according to this view, there are surpluses of births and the population may grow quite rapidly but, since the productive capacity of the community cannot match its power of demographic increase, each such interlude of growth is terminated by a mortality surge which may wipe out the gains of a generation in a matter of months.
>
> Yet England patently did not conform to the high-pressure paradigm. An accommodation between population and resources was secured not by sudden, sharp mortality spasms, but by wide, quiet fluctuations in fertility, which in their downward phase reduced fertility levels to the point where population growth ceased even though mortality was still low by the standards of other pre-industrial societies. In contrast to the mortality-dominated high-pressure equilibrium sometimes regarded as generally present in all pre-industrial societies, England experienced a fertility-dominated low-pressure system. (Wrigley and Schofield 1981:450-451.)

Without presupposing what will ultimately be found to be the case for Mesopotamia, it is clearly a matter of interest beyond the limits of demographic history to assess  where, along the continuum between these two contrastive models, Mesopotamian society lay in different periods. To do this, data will be needed on questions that presently receive little attention: age and age-differences at marriage, numbers of offspring per family, lengths of generational intervals, seasonality of death from natural causes, relative proportions of extended and nuclear households, and short-term variations in urban density. All of these appear to be at least partially amenable to Assyriological or archaeological investigation, although no doubt this will require considerable improvements in existing methods and an enlargement in the supply of data to sustain a shift toward more systematic, quantitative analysis.

## Urbanism, technology and the political economy

Thus far I have dealt primarily with economic questions that may be investigated with textual sources and which link to demographic trends disclosed by archaeological surveys. It should not be overlooked that the same survey data reveal equally striking and consistent shifts over time in settlement size and distribution. Admittedly these shifts can be seen at present only through a screen of arbitrarily bounded size categories that probably do not reflect distinct residential or socially recognized gradations. But the underlying trends would not be obscured by any units of measurement. There was a decline in the proportion of the settled area that was unambiguously urban from 78 percent to 16 percent during the course of the late third and second millennia (Table 1). An even steeper rise to the earlier, higher level may have occurred during the late fourth and early third millennia. Tendencies toward rural dispersal into villages and small towns are almost exactly the reverse of these, while settlements of intermediate size remain relatively stable as a proportion of the total. One obvious question suggested by these trends is whether the interplay of supply and demand factors with demographic trends could also have been linked to major, long-term changes in the extent of urbanism. Two possible connections suggest themselves.

The first emerges from a fairly strictly economic approach:

Urban areas are a particular spatial ordering of economic activity which have both associated benefits and costs. The gains accrue to those activities which benefit particularly from proximity to transportation nodes or specialized supply services. The costs come in the form of higher land prices and, frequently, congestion. This produces a natural division of activities between the city and the countryside. Those activities such as merchandising, financial services, and certain types of manufacturing, to whom the benefits from urban locations outweigh their costs naturally locate in cities. Those activities where the sensitivity to land cost is very important, such as agriculture or forestry, must operate in nonurban areas. A corollary of this urban/rural division which is most important for this study is that new or innovative activities tend to be most advantageously sited in urban areas. There they have access to special production and marketing skills, an advantage which at this stage more than offset the higher production costs of the city. As the production techniques of a given product are developed and standardized, however, the lower cost structure of production in the countryside becomes a strong drawing factor. (Gunderson 1976:57.)

Transferred from "declining" Rome to Mesopotamia, this line of argument might maintain that the ongoing technological changes suggested earlier for third millennium agriculture, together with others affecting the organization of craft production or commodity distribution, initially gave great economic advantages to growing urban centers. This might have been a major factor in the condition of apparent hyper-urbanization existing by the mid-third millennium B.C. In time, however, these relative advantages declined as the innovations on which they were based diffused outward to smaller towns and villages, and indeed, to regions outside the Mesopotamian alluvium. Meanwhile urban disadvantages were beginning to accrue, connected, for example, with the progressive salinization of the lowest, longest and most intensively urbanized portion of the Mesopotamian plain. Similarly, as the technological and adminstrative infrastructures for the exercise of political and military power became more widely dispersed, the inherent vulnerability of downstream water-users to upstream mismanagement or diversions became a progressively more important factor. This growing vulnerability is clear in the historic record, expanding the concern beyond the strictly economic issues that have been explored heretofore into the larger, less regularity-prone sphere of the political economy. A second possibility for explaining changes in urbanism lies there.

By no later than the early third millennium urban settlements in ancient Mesopotamia were frequently, perhaps universally, enclosed by walls. Their architecturally impressive defenses are consistent with other evidence of militarism. Costly and technically sophisticated armaments are well represented in tomb furnishings. There are numerous representations of battle scenes. And cuneiform texts attest not only to elaborate military organizations but to the destructiveness of warfare. Walled cities, one can therefore argue, were only one part of military activities that once again would profit by being viewed in systems terms. The ostensible purpose of the system as a whole presumably was the protection of urban populations, including their stored agricultural reserves and other forms of wealth, and, in a symbolic sense, the city-temple residences of their patron deities. But the whole apparatus could equally well be mobilized for expansion and aggrandizement. In any case, the formation of cities, and not simply their fortification and the regimentation of their inhabitants, is clearly part of the same system. Urban nucleation involved the abandonment of less defensible smaller settlements, and the creation of much more potent offensive and defensive concentrations of paramilitary personnel and their provisioners and dependents.

This militaristic development demanded the commitment of a large share of social resources, as unfortunately it still does today. Perhaps we can assume that greater security was made possible thereby, although it is no less likely that offensive and defensive capabilities more or less kept pace with one another. And the escalating cost in taxes and in involuntary military and labor service was high, not to speak of upward income transfers associated with increasing social stratification that surely went on more rapidly within the cities than in the more subsistence-oriented settlements that preceded them. Without suggesting that the trade-offs of urbanization remained constant, it seems certain that they were at most times differently perceived by urban elites, who were the principal beneficiaries of the system, than by the mass of the ordinary population. The Gilgamesh Epic is set in motion, after all, by the protests of Uruk's citizenry to the gods over the enormous labor involved in the construction of that city's wall. Or again, the militia sometimes had to be employed in pursuing and repatriating former neighbors who had sought to escape from urban life into the rural hinterlands. This is hardly surprising, since at least the military strength of a city would have been enhanced by maintaining a large and stable population. But it follows that complementary 'push' and 'pull' factors—the attractions of security and proximity to religious and commercial foci, and on the other hand also measures of coercion—probably were involved in the formation of cities out of preceding grids of smaller towns and villages. While primarily of a defensive character, city walls can be viewed in at least a symbolic sense as walls of inclusion as well as exclusion.

This view of the rise of urbanism emphasizes underlying clashes of interest between adjacent communities and different social strata. Presumably these stemmed in large part from differences, whether in opportunity or merely in perception, over access to desirable land, water, raw materials, stored reserves, and the like. Also involved may have been a degree of structural and ideological tension between traditional, theocratically based elites in the older cities and the more politically and militaristically oriented (but only in a very qualified sense more 'secular') leadership in centers whose rapid rise to urban status took place somewhat later (Charvát 1981). For either reason, intercity rivalries were openly expressed and vigorously pursued. On the other hand, it is unclear whether intracommunity antagonisms along essentially class lines ever were perceived or acted upon.

Johannes Renger has observed that "[a]s far as we know, the

tension in Mesopotamian society never developed to such a degree that the existence of the social organization as such would have been in jeopardy—neither through passive resistance, nor flight, nor especially through open rebellion" (1972:180). However, the qualification "as far as we know" is a significant one. As already pointed out, the cuneiform texts all but exclusively embody the perceptions and concerns of urban elites. There is little or no scope for the recording of oppositional activities or contrary viewpoints. Moreover, groups can pursue strategies that are objectively at variance with one another irrespective of whether their differences were consciously recognized. It seems at least as reasonable to assume that differential access to resources or exposure to risk and deprivation contributed to the formation of intracommunity groupings with different loyalties and objectives as to assume that the entire society voluntarily and unformly embraced the mythopoeic traditions that sanctioned the political as well as the divine order.

There is no necessary contradiction between the conflict-uncertainty-and-variance mode of explanation just outlined for the rise of Mesopotamian urbanism and the economy-and-technology mode that was sketched previously. Both probably have parts to play within a still more comprehensive causal framework. In fact, they tend to converge as we move on to the long decline in the proportion of urban settlement that began in its original heartland in the late third millennium. Mention has already been made of salinization and downstream vulnerability. The movement of urban primacy and political authority upstream to Babylon that unquestionably undermined the viability of the older configuration of settlement on the lower plain is consistent with both avenues of explanation. A widespread, abrupt cessation in the production of dated clay tablets suggests that the major southern centers were substantially abandoned soon after 1740 B.C. (Stone 1977), and as a consequence of this there may well have been a northward exodus of population to newly developing districts in the hinterlands of Babylon. There has been essentially no archaeological attention to outlying or smaller settlements, so that we do not know how those of the later second millennium in the south differed structurally from the larger cities that then lay in ruins around them. Possibly there had been a drift in the direction of greater reliance on pastoralism, a form of land use that may even have been optimal in districts badly affected by salinity. But possibly also the dispersion of formerly urban-based organizational and technological skills (including even the scribal art?) had proceeded to the point where these could be sustained in relatively modest but fully sedentary villages. While many details are still obscure, it seems likely that at least some major aspects of urbanism's evolving pattern can be brought within the same broad, causal nexus as the demographic and supply and demand factors discussed earlier.

### The Undeveloped Study of Changing Gender Relationships

This account of prospective themes around which humanistic and anthropological approaches to the evolution of Mesopotamian society can and should be integrated in the years ahead can only be left incomplete. Additional candidates, while numerous, cannot yet be delineated in comparable detail. But deserving at least brief mention is one that is closely related, and potentially even more challenging. It concerns the position of women, with interregional trade and warfare providing the connecting links.

Long-distance trade was vital in securing raw materials in which the Mesopotamian alluvium was wholly deficient. Among them were copper, tin, and precious metals for cultic purposes and sumptuary display and more importantly for armaments. No less critical was timber suitable for monumental building, furniture, carts and chariots, and especially ship and barge construction, because the agricultural economies of the greatly enlarged third millennium cities were heavily dependent on Gulf commerce, fishing, and riverine transport. Key resources could not be obtained on a reliable basis simply by sending expeditions to extract them as booty—although periodically this was also done. Their consistent supply in adequate amounts required an established fabric of trading relations, and this in turn required large-scale production of commodities for export.

With regard to early and mid-third millennium warfare, some discount is certainly plausible in claims of casualties and representations of its ferocity. But by all accounts it was sanguinary. Heaps of dead are said to have been left on battlefields, and there are strong suggestions that many more soldiers in vanquished armies were put to the sword after victory rather than taken prisoner. Male prisoners of war who are so specified in administrative texts rather than in formalized (and probably inflated) victory claims are relatively few. On the other hand, it appears virtually certain that additional male prisoners were blinded to inhibit their mobility and then employed as gardeners or millers (Gelb 1973:74, 87; Diakonoff 1974:70-71). This practice appears to have declined after Early Dynastic times, at the same time as references begin to the mass deportation of whole communities of defeated enemies.

A plausible reconstruction of the circumstances behind these practices is that, under conditions of internecine warfare among neighboring city states, male prisoners might be frequently taken but were difficult to employ productively because of the ease of escape. Hence some were blinded and used in the limited capacities that this permitted, but most were killed. This may have become less of a problem with the greater stability and territorial extent of dynastic domains in the last third millennium. By then, moreover, the practice of forcibly transporting whole communities would have reduced inducements to escape. Alternatives to the killing or blinding of male prisoners thus gradually became more practical.

In the case of female prisoners, however, the obstacles to productive use were never so serious. They were seized in very large numbers, frequently with their children, and the texts attest that they were employed primarily in the production of textiles under quasi-industrial conditions. Imports of textiles from distant centers like Ebla also are known (Foster 1977:39), but on balance

they must have constituted Mesopotamia's major export product—the only one with a sufficiently high value-to-weight ratio
to sustain long-distance overland as well as maritime commerce on
a scale matching Mesopotamia's need for external resources. Thus
the growth in intensity of Mesopotamian warfare, coupled with
efforts to rationalize procurement of the raw materials that were
vital to the growing cities, introduced a stream of dependent or
enslaved women directly into the cities. That this prolonged, large-
scale phenomenon would have had pervasive effects on the entire
social system, but especially on the status of women, to me seems
beyond dispute.

Unfortunately, it is not yet possible to detect these effects
unambiguously in either archaeological or textual sources. While
seemingly the more promising place to look, genres of cuneiform
texts that might record such information are not sufficiently
numerous or informative until after the processes described above
had been underway for centuries. There are rare cases in early
documents of matronyms as well as patronyms, and of descent
associated with land tenure being traced through females as well
as males. Women occasionally appear among the "lords of the
field" in sale contracts, and as heads of single-parent households
on ration lists. Save perhaps for the king himself, monogamy
prevailed everywhere (Gelb 1979:26, 28, 36, 61, 78, 89). Sumerian proverbs provide evidence of the active inculcation of female
submissiveness, a likely adjunct to an ongoing erosion of status:

> A rebellious male may be permitted a reconciliation (?);
> A rebellious female will be dragged in the mud (Gordon 1959:
> 123).

Out of such limited indications as these one might fashion a
trend that led over time toward the well-established patriarchal
households that are richly attested in the early-to-mid-second
millennium in numerous private letters and in the law code of
Hammurabi. Even at that time some women, apparently disposing
of the pooled capital resources of their families although they

operated from a cloistered setting, were able to play a central part in business affairs (Harris 1964; Stone 1982). Arguably, the sanction given to their activities originated at an earlier time when women's roles were less circumscribed. The survival for even longer of a female deity like Nisaba as the patroness of the scribal art also may hint at a quite different gender configuration at around the outset of the third millennium or somewhat earlier. All this is still frankly speculative. What I will insist upon is only that some substantial erosion in female status seems probable in light of the conditions in the political economy that have been described—and that systematically setting aside our preconceptions and developing new ways of reconstructing what the antecedent patterns were is a challenge that scholars should no longer ignore. It illustrates once again a potentially productive association between new themes of investigation and those very broad and transformative changes for which only the term evolution seems wholly appropriate.

## Constructionism, Reductionism, and the Utility of a Darwinian Prototype

In conclusion, it is perhaps worth asking in what respects an approach concerning itself in admittedly somewhat eclectic, transdisciplinary ways with cultural, social, and economic history can be described as evolutionary. Certainly the differences from classical Darwinism are rather striking, although Darwinism, too, is currently subject to a critical reformulation. As Stephen Gould has recently written, "the essence of Darwinism lies in a claim that natural selection is the primary directing force of evolution, in that it creates fitter phenotypes by differently preserving, generation by generation, the best adapted organisms from a pool of random variants that supply raw material only, not direction itself" (1982:381).

In the paths of social evolution with which this paper has concerned itself, by contrast, it is socioculturally constituted groups and not individual organisms that are the units of selection. Nor are the most significant of such groups, from the perspective of identifying forces primarily responsible for particular changes, generally coterminous with whole populations or societies. Variations, moreover, need not be random. Goal oriented, even experimentally derived, variation in response to differently experienced hazard and opportunity is characteristic of complex societies and may even be common in "primitive" ones. The adoption of novelties often therefore depends less on selection through differential survival or reproduction rates than on the active efforts of groups associated with them. Further, social evolution cannot be thought of as a holistic process. While recent archaeological advances rest to a considerable extent on the faith that there is an intimate and discoverable linkage between material findings and the organizational and symbolic structures that originally held them in place, there are, as Friedman (above, p. 87) insists, numerous dimensions of both meaning and action that for long periods could remain relatively independent of one another. And the units of social change are never clearly bounded in the sense that (at least at any given moment in time) genetically defined populations are. In fact, a study of change in human societies is inconceivable without recognition of their openness along every frontier of interaction.

What then is left of classical Darwinism in the characteristics I would ascribe to social evolution? Philip Anderson, a Nobelist in physics, provides a thoughtful statement of the difficulties involved in any transfer of substance across a gulf like that between the biological and the cultural realms:

> The ability to reduce everything to simple fundamental laws does not imply the ability to start from those laws and reconstruct the universe. . . . The constructionist hypothesis breaks down when confronted with the twin difficulties of scale and complexity. The behavior of large and complex aggregates of elementary particles, it turns out, is not to be understood in terms of a simple extrapolation of the properties of a few particles. Instead, at each new level of complexity entirely new

properties appear, and the understanding of the new behaviors requires research which I think is as fundamental in its nature as any other. (Anderson 1972:393)

Those who pursue the goal of a "science of men [and women] in time," whether as historians, archaeologists, anthropologists, or even in some cases as humanists,[1] thus should recognize that sociocultural development must first be understood in its own terms. Biologists share our concern for understanding how and why structures are transformed over time, how they form aggregates, and how they interact both as individuals and as aggregates. An eco-system framework (although hardly Darwinian), can be a common starting point. Although its cultural manifestations are necessarily more open, partial and ambiguously defined than its biological ones. But essentially no help in understanding the transitions of interest to us should be expected from analogies with mechanisms of biological change.

Perhaps there is another bridge to biological evolutionism, slender but enduring. There is an embracing epistemological similarity of outlooks, even if the phenomena with which we deal are organized in sets and levels with their own autonomous properties. As in the natural sciences more generally, those involved in tracing the evolution of culture tend to be aligned on the formally explanatory, "laws-and-instances," rather than "cases-and-interpretations," side of the diffuse polarity (or complementarity) in the social sciences that Geertz (1980) has sketched. We

[1] Henry Wright (personal communication) points out that Marc Bloch's "science" is better translated as "scholarly study" than as "science" in its English usage. The same applies, of course, to the meaning of the German "Wissenschaft." But a fundamental, if heretofore largely implicit, premise of this paper is that the French and German usage is preferable to our own—that ultimately there is an irregular continuum rather than a sharp break between scientific explanation and humanistic understanding. See now the suggestive treatment of this subject by R. W. Fogel (in press). I am much indebted to Wright, as well as to John A. Brinkman, for a close reading and some very penetrating criticisms of the penultimate draft of this paper.

gravitate toward studies of what ultimately proved to be decisive, irreversible advances in the human career, such as the new constellations of features following in the wake of food production or accompanying the rise of urban civilization. Yet even as we assert this hierarchy of priorities, we find it more and more necessary to acknowledge and learn from the indeterminacy and reversibility of short-term change and the not infrequent immunity to change of underlying structures of thought and action.

Finally, the scope of changes to which an evolutionary approach seems appropriate is so large as to invite, if not demand, comparative study. What is sought in this way is not merely a higher-level synthesis of instances that naturally differ in many specific details, but also a measure of the adequacy of our understanding of recurrent, transformative processes. This turns our attention away from a recitation of similarities and differences in more or less independent sequences of more or less homotaxial stages.[2] As the idea of a succession of holistic, "total" systems

---

[2] Wright's comment on this statement offers a possible theme for a future symposium:

> It is hard to decide what is "recurrent" if one doesn't have the standard of comparability insured by a stage system. If you lack comparability and get transformative sequences misaligned, one sees differences between developments where they are not so marked. For example in your 1966 book (Adams 1966), you compared the rather sophisticated third-generation Aztec polity—probably best compared to Rim-Sin's Larsa or Hammurabi's Babylon with their professional armies, garrisons, merchants, multiple monetary standards, etc.--with the first-generation empire of Sargon of Agade. You did this because the complexity of Teotihuacan and of its Middle and Late Formative predecessors was simply not recognized at the time you wrote the book, ... but it seems to me that this unavoidable misalignment helped to create the seeming contrast between what you termed "step" and "ramp" careers and to mask some other, perhaps more interesting, contrasts between Mesoamerica and the Old World civilizations. For sure, I am as against the recitation and refinement of stage systems for their own sake as you are. But they do serve useful purposes in comparative studies: We cannot consider variations except in a context where similarities are controlled (and vice versa of course). This is why I bridle when I hear what seem to be attacks on any interest in stage systems.

seems progressively less tenable, so for comparative purposes our attention must focus instead on loosely intersecting, competing, co-existing, semi-autonomous, and often long-enduring sub-systems. And what is most of interest is the *variability* (rather than the regularity or predictability of response) of these sub-systems to circumstances that were differently perceived and experienced. Of course, this does not deny the utility of detailed comparisons. But the analytical thrust is toward disaggregation and concrete instantiation, rather than toward least-common-denominator abstraction.

Evolutionary strategies are no more static than anything else. The possibilities sketched out here may in some respects extend processes of modification that have been underway for as long as social scientists have entertained such strategies. But it should also be evident that there are strong, underlying elements of continuity. In short, taken in sufficiently broad and flexible terms, an evolutionary approach continues to be fruitful.

**References**

Adams, R. McC.

1966     *The evolution of urban society: Early Mesopotamia and prehispanic Mexico*. Chicago: Aldine.

1981     *Heartland of cities: Surveys of ancient settlement and land use on the central floodplain of the Euphrates*. Chicago: University of Chicago Press.

1982a    Die Rolle des Bewässerungsbodenbaus bei der Entwicklung von Institutionen in der altmesopotamischen Gesellschaft. In *Produktivkräfte und Gesellschaftsformationen in vorkapitalistischer Zeit*, edited by J. Herrmann and I. Sellnow, pp. 119-140. Berlin: Akademie-Verlag.

1982b    Property rights and functional tenure in Mesopotamian rural communities. In *Societies and languages of the ancient Near East: Studies in honour of I. M.*

*Diakonoff*, edited by M. A. Dandamayev et al., pp. 1-14. London: Aris and Phillips.

Anderson, P. W.
1972     More is different. *Science* 177:393-396.

Anonymous
1982     Chemical methods reveal diet of early humans. *Chemical and Engineering News*, January 25, 1982: 31-35.

Barth, F.
1966     Anthropological models and social reality. *Proceedings of the Royal Society* 165:20-34.

Binford, L. R.
1972     *An archaeological perspective.* New York: Seminar Press.
1981     Behavioral archaeology and the 'Pompeii premise'. *Journal of Anthropological Research* 37:195-208.

Bloch, M.
1964     *The historian's craft.* New York: Random House.

Braudel, F.
1972     History and the social sciences. In *Economy and society in early modern Europe: Essays from Annales*, edited by P. Burke, pp. 11-42.

Brenner, R., et al.
1977-    Agrarian class structure and economic development
1978     in pre-industrial Europe. *Past and Present* 70:3-75, with discussion in nos. 78-80.

Charvát, P.
1981     The Kish evidence and the emergence of states in Mesopotamia. *Current Anthropology* 22:686-688.

Cipolla, C. M.
1980     *Before the Industrial Revolution.* New York: W. W. Norton, 2nd ed.

Civil, M.
  1980    Les limites de l'information textuelle. In *L'archéologie de l'Iraq: perspectives et limites de l'interpretation anthropologique des documents,* pp. 225-232. Colloques internationaux du C.N.R.S. Paris.

Desrochers, M. J.
  1978    *Aspects of the structure of Dilbat during the Old Babylonian period.* Unpublished Ph.D. diss., University of California at Los Angeles.

Diakonoff, I. M.
  1972    Socio-economic classes in Babylonia and the Babylonian concept of social stratification. In *Gesellschaftsklassen im Alten Zweistromland und in den angrenzenden Gebieten—XVIII. Rencontre assyriologique internationale,* edited by D. O. Edzard, pp. 41-52.
  1974    Slaves, helots and serfs in early antiquity. *Academiae Scientarum Hungaricae, Acta Antiqua* 22: 45-78.

Falkenstein, A.
  1954    La cité-temple sumérienne. *Cahiers d'Histoire Mondiale* 1:784-814.

Farber, H.
  1978    A price and wage study for northern Babylonia during the Old Babylonian period. *Journal of the Economic and Social History of the Orient* 21:1-51.

Flannery, K. V.
  1972    The cultural evolution of civilizations. *Annual Review of Ecology and Systematics* 3:399-426.

Fogel, R. W.
  In        Circumstantial evidence in 'scientific' and tradi-
  press.   tional history. In *Philosophy of history and contemporary historiography,* edited by David Carr et al. Ottawa: Uniersity of Ottawa Press.

124          *Robert McC. Adams*

Foster, B. R.
  1977    Commercial activity in Sargonic Mesopotamia. *Iraq* 23:31-43.

Friedman, J.
  1974    Marxism, structuralism and vulgar materialism. *Man* 9:444-469.

Geertz, C.
  1980    Blurred genres. *American Scholar* 49:165-179.

Gelb, I. J.
  1969    On the alleged temple and state economies in another Mesopotamia. In *Studi in Onore di Edoardo Volterra,* vol. 6, pp. 137-154. Rome.
  1973    Prisoners of war in early Mesopotamia. *Journal of Near Eastern Studies* 32:70-98.
  1979    Household and family in early Mesopotamia. In State and temple economy in the ancient Near East, edited by E. Lipinski. *Orientalia Louvaniensia Analecta* 5:1-99.

Gibson, McG.
  1974    Violation of fallow and engineered disaster in Mesopotamian civilization. In Irrigation's impact on society. *University of Arizona, Anthropological Papers,* 25:7-20, edited by T. D. Downing and McG. Gibson.

Gilman, A.
  1981    The development of social stratification in Bronze Age Europe. *Current Anthropology* 22:1-23.

Gledhill, J., and M. Larsen
  1982    The Polanyi paradigm and a dynamic analysis of archaic states. In *Theory and explanation in archaeology: The Southampton Conference,* edited by C. Renfrew, M. J. Rowlands and B. A. Segraves, pp. 197-229. New York: Academic Press.

Gordon, E. I.
1959    *Sumerian proverbs: Glimpses of everyday life in ancient Mesopotamia.* Philadelphia: Museum Monographs.

Gould, S. J.
1982    Darwinism and the expansion of evolutionary theory. *Science* 216:380-387.

Gunderson, G.
1976    Economic change and the demise of the Roman empire. *Explorations in Economic History* 13:43-68.

Harris, R.
1964    The Naditu woman. In *Studies presented to A. Leo Oppenheim*, pp. 106-135. Chicago: University of Chicago Press.

Hilton, R. H.
1975    *The English peasantry in the later Middle Ages.* Oxford: Clarendon Press.

Jacobsen, T.
1953    The reign of Ibbi-Suen. *Journal of Cuneiform Studies* 7:36-47.

Jacobsen, T., and R. McC. Adams
1958    Salt and silt in ancient Mesopotamian agriculture. *Science* 128:1251-1258.

Jakobson, V. A.
1971    Some problems connected with the rise of landed property (Old Babylonian period). *Beiträge zur sozialen Struktur des alten Vorderasien*, edited by H. Klengel, pp. 33-37.

Kamp, K. A., and N. Yoffee
1980    Ethnicity in ancient western Asia during the early second millennium B.C.: Archaeological assessments and ethno-archaeological prospectives. *Bulletin of the American Schools of Oriental Research* 237: 85-104.

Klengel, H.
1971    Soziale Aspekte der altbabylonischen Dienstmiete. In *Beiträge zur sozialen Struktur des alten Vorderasien*, edited by H. Klengel, pp. 39-52. Berlin: Akademie Verlag.

Kramer, S. N.
1969    The curse of Agade. In *Ancient Near Eastern texts related to the Old Testament*, edited by J. B. Pritchard, pp. 646-651. 3rd ed. Princeton: Princeton University Press.

Kuhn, T. S.
1970    *The structure of scientific revolutions.* 2nd ed. Chicago: University of Chicago Press.

Kula, W.
1976    *An economic theory of the feudal system: toward a model of the Polish economy 1500-1800.* London: NLB.

Lambert, M.
1953    La vie économique de Shuruppak. *Sumer* 9:198-213.

1963    L'usage de l'argent métal à Lagash au temps de la 3ᵉ Dynastie d'Ur. *Revue d'Assyriologie* 57:79-92, 193-200.

Larsen, M. T.
1976    The Old Assyrian city-state and its colonies. *Mesopotamia* 4. Copenhagen: Akademisk Forlag.

Leach, E. R.
1973    Concluding address. In *The explanation of culture change: models in prehistory*, edited by C. Renfrew. London: Duckworth.

Le Roy Ladurie, E.
1974    *The peasants of Languedoc.* Urbana: University of Illinois Press.

Maekawa, K.
1973- The development of the é-mí in Lagash during Early
1974 Dynastic III. *Mesopotamia* 8-9:77-144.

Marfoe, L.
1980 The integrative transformation: Patterns of socio-
political organization in southern Syria. *Bulletin of
the American Schools of Oriental Research* 234:
1-42.

Michalowski, P.
1978 The Neo-Sumerian ring texts. *Syro-Mesopotamian
Studies* 2:43-58.

Muhly, J. D.
1981 Review of J. D. Hawkins, ed., Trade in the Ancient
Near East—XXIII Rencontre Assyriologique internationale. *Journal of the American Oriental Society*
100:173-175.

Nissen, H. J.
1976 Geographie. In *Sumerological studies in honor of
Thorkild Jacobsen*, edited by S. J. Lieverman, pp.
9-40. *Assyriological Studies* 20. Chicago: University of Chicago Press.

Oppenheim, A. L.
1957 A bird's-eye view of Mesopotamian economic history. In K. Polanyi, C. M. Arensberg, and H. W.
Pearson 1957, pp. 27-37.
1964 *Ancient Mesopotamia: Portrait of a dead civilization.* Chicago: University of Chicago Press.

Polanyi, K., C. M. Arensberg, and H. W. Pearson
1957 *Trade and markets in the early empires.* Glencoe:
Free Press and Falcon's Wing Press.

Postan, M. M.
1975 *The medieval economy and society.* Harmonds-
worth: Pelican.

Powell, M. A.
　1977　Sumerian merchants and the problem of profit. *Iraq*
　　　　23:23-29.

　1978　A contribution to the history of money in Mesopo-
　　　　tamia prior to the invention of coinage. *Assyriologia*
　　　　5:211-241 Budapest.

Renger, J.
　1972　Flucht als soziales Problem in der altbabylonischen
　　　　Gesellschaft. In *Gesellschaftsklassen im Alten Zwei-
　　　　stromland und in den angrenzended Gebieten—
　　　　XVIII. Rencontre assyriologique internationale*,
　　　　edited by D. O. Edzard, pp. 167-182. Bayerische
　　　　Akademie der Wissenschaften, Phil.-Hist. Klasse,
　　　　*Abhandlungen*, N.F. 75.

　In　　Patterns of non-institutional trade and non-com-
　press.　mercial exchange in ancient Mesopotamia at the
　　　　beginning of the second millennium B.C. *Studi
　　　　Micenei ed Egeo-Anatolici* 25.

Robertson, J. F.
　1981　*Redistributive economies in ancient Mesopotamian
　　　　society: a case study from Isin-Larsa period Nippur.*
　　　　Ph.D. dissertation, University of Pennsylvania.

Sauren, H.
　1966　*Topographie der Provinz Umma nach den Urkunden
　　　　der Zeit der III. Dynastie von Ur. Teil I. Känale und
　　　　Bewässerungsanlagen.* Ph.D. dissertation, Ruprecht-
　　　　Karl Universität zu Heidelberg.

Schoeninger, M. J.
　1981　The agricultural 'revolution': Its effect on human
　　　　diet in prehistoric Iran and Israel. *Paléorient* 7:
　　　　73-91.

Snell, D. C.
　1982　*Ledgers and prices: Early Mesopotamian merchant
　　　　accounts.* Yale Near Eastern Researches, 8. New
　　　　Haven: Yale University Press.

Stolper, M.
1974    *Management and politics in late Achaemenid Baby-
        lonia: New texts from the Murasu archive.* Unpub-
        lished Ph.D. dissertation, University of Michigan.

Stone, E. C.
1977    Economic crisis and social upheaval in Old Babylo-
        nian Nippur. In *Mountains and lowlands: essays in
        the archaeology of greater Mesopotamia,* edited by
        L. D. Levine and T. C. Young, Jr., pp. 267-289.
        *Bibliotheca Mesopotamica* 7. Malibu: Undena.
1982    The social role of the naditu women in Old Babylo-
        nian Nippur. *Journal of the Economic and Social
        History of the Orient* 25:50-70.

Stone, L.
1972    *The causes of the English Revolution 1529-1642.*
        New York: Harper and Row.

Sweet, R. F. G.
1958    *On prices, moneys and money uses in the Old Baby-
        lonian period.* Ph.D. dissertation, University of
        Chicago.

Veenhof, K. R.
1972    *Aspects of Old Assyrian trade and its terminology.*
        Studia det Documenta ad Iura Orientis Antiqui Per-
        tinentia 10. Leiden: Brill.

Wittfogel, K. A.
1957    *Oriental Despotism: a comparative study of total
        power.* New Haven: Yale University Press.

Wrigley, E. A., and R. S. Schofield
1981    *The population history of England 1541-1871: a
        reconstruction.* Cambridge: Harvard University
        Press.

Yoffee, N.
1981    Explaining trade in ancient western Asia. *Mono-
        graphs on the Ancient Near East* 2:21-60. Malibu:
        Undena.

# OUR CONTRIBUTORS

**WILLIAM T. SANDERS** is a Professor of Anthropology, Pennsylvania State University. He received his Ph.D. from Harvard University in 1957 and has conducted field research in Mexico, Guatemala, and Honduras. Primary research interests are cultural ecology, prehistoric demography, and the evolution of civilization in Mesoamerica. His publications include *Cultural Ecology of the Teotihuacan Valley* (1965), *Mesoamerica: the Evolution of a Civilization* (with B. J. Price, 1968), *Teotihuacan and Kaminaljuyu: a Study in Prehistoric Culture Contact* (with J. W. Michels, 1977), and *The Basin of Mexico: Ecological Processes in the Evolution of a Civilization* (with J. R. Parsons and R. S. Santley, 1979).

**HENRY T. WRIGHT** is a Curator of Archaeology, Museum of Anthropology, University of Michigan. He received his Ph.D. from the University of Chicago in 1967 and has conducted field research in various parts of North America, Europe, the Near East, East Africa, and most recently on Madagascar and the Comoro Islands. One of his research interests has been the evolution of states. Among his publications relevant to this issue are *The Administration of Rural Production in an Early Mesopotamian Town* (1969), "Population, Exchange, and Early State Formation in Southwestern Iran" (with G. Johnson, 1975), "Recent Research on the Origin of the State" (1977), "Time and Process in an Uruk Rural Community" (with N. Miller and R. Redding, 1980), and *An Early Town on the Deh Luran Plain* (1981).

**ROBERT McC. ADAMS** is Harold H. Swift Distinguished Service Professor of Anthropology, Director of the Oriental Institute, and Provost, University of Chicago. He received his Ph.D. there in 1956 and has conducted field research in Mexico, Iran, Syria, Saudi Arabia, and especially in Iraq. Primary among his research concerns is the tracing of secular, ecological, demographic, and economic trends in the urban-agrarian civilizations of the proto-historic and historic Near East. His publications include *Land Behind Baghdad* (1965), *The Evolution of Urban Society* (1966), *The Uruk Countryside* (with H. J. Nissen, 1972), and *Heartland of Cities* (1981).

# THE EDITOR

**TIMOTHY EARLE** is an associate professor of anthropology, UCLA. He received his Ph.D. from the University of Michigan in 1973. He has conducted field research in the Hawaiian Islands and is presently directing an archaeological project in Peru. His research interests include the evolution of complex societies, prehistoric economics, and cultural ecology. Among his publications are *Exchange Systems in Prehistory* (with J. Ericson, 1977), *Economic and Social Organization of a Complex Chiefdom* (1978), *Modeling Change in Prehistoric Subsistence Economies* (with A. Christenson, 1980), and *Contexts for Prehistoric Exchange* (with J. Ericson, 1982).